JOURNALISM ETHICS

MICHAEL KRONENWETTER

JOURNALISM
ETHICS

FRANKLIN WATTS / 1988
NEW YORK / LONDON / TORONTO / SYDNEY
AN IMPACT BOOK

Photographs courtesy of:
AP/Wide World Photos: pp. 15, 76; ROTHCO Cartoons: pp.
35, 55, 57, 64, 69, 82, 85, 88, 94, 110; Photo Researchers:
p. 60 (Bettye Lane); New York Post: p. 100 (Paul Adao).

Library of Congress Cataloging-in-Publication Data

Kronenwetter, Michael.

Journalism ethics / Michael Kronenwetter.

p. cm.—(An Impact book)
Bibliography: p.
Includes index.
Summary: Examines the issue of journalistic ethics, discussing
such areas as accuracy, conflicts of interest, relationships with
sources, and slanting the news.
ISBN 0-531-10589-X
1. Journalistic ethics—Juvenile literature. [1. Journalistic
ethics.] I. Title.
PN4797.K7 1988
174'.9097—dc19   88-5478   CIP   AC

CONTENTS

JOURNALISM ETHICS

1

THE POWER
AND PERVASIVENESS
OF THE NEWS MEDIA

The mass media—newspapers, magazines, radio, and television—are pervasive in American society today. They are everywhere.

There are over 9,000 newspapers in the United States, including some 1,700 dailies. According to the latest available figures, over 63 million copies of these papers are distributed each day, along with millions of copies of magazines. Experts estimate that the number of people who actually read all these publications is much larger, because the average copy is read by more than one reader.

Along with the print press, there are more than 1,500 television stations and almost 10,000 radio stations, which reach even more Americans every day. Fully 99 percent of American households have radios, and most of them have more than one. Almost 85 percent of these households also have television sets. There's no way to tell how many people are listening to and watching all these sets, nor for how long, but the average television household has at least one set turned on more than seven hours each and every day.

Each of these media of communication ("media" is the

plural of "medium") devotes a significant amount of its efforts to journalism—the dissemination of more or less current news, information, and ideas to the public. Most newspapers and newsmagazines, like *Time* and *Newsweek*, give over most of their pages to journalism; many other publications, not primarily devoted to journalism, often feature articles that fall into that category.

All three major commercial television networks have large and active news departments that produce daily news shows, along with other news and public events programming; at least three cable television networks devote themselves entirely to news-related programming. Individual television stations often put most of their production efforts into their own, local news shows. That is because these are often the stations' highest-rated local programs, and the ones that bring in the most money from local sponsors.

The Public Broadcasting System, which doesn't rely on sponsors, produces an hour-long daily news show, and broadcasts a number of other journalism-related programs as well.

Because of their roles as purveyors of journalism, the mass media are often referred to jointly as the "news media." And because of their pervasiveness, most Americans are exposed to several examples of journalism every day, whether they want to be or not.

It is through the news media that most of us get much of our information, as well as many of our ideas. Back in the days when the newspaper was the only major news medium, the entertainer Will Rogers used to say that all he knew was what he read in the papers. Expanded to include the electronic media as well, his comment could be applied today to American society as a whole.

DISSEMINATING NEWS
AND OPINIONS

It is through the news media that the majority of us learn most of what we know about the contemporary world

**METS GET
THE MAGIC BACK**

**WORKER IS KILLED
IN NUCLEAR LEAK**

**A TAX BILL FOR
THE TEXTBOOKS**

**AMERICAN HELD IN
LEBANON IS FREED**

**NATION REKINDLES STATUE OF
LIBERTY AS BEACON OF HOPE**

**MOOSE'S LOVE TAKES
A PLACE IN LITERATURE**

**YUPPIES, IT'S
ALL OVER...**

**GORBY MAKES STOP
TO PRESS THE FLESH**

*Newspapers contain all kinds of news,
as these headlines demonstrate.*

beyond our personal experience. Without the media, most Americans would have little knowledge of what life is like for the people who live in other neighborhoods of their own cities, much less for the people in other nations of the world. Without the media, we would only find out about major world happenings—from earthquakes to famines, from the results of the Olympic games to the results of distant wars—long after the events occurred. With the media, thanks to today's satellite technology, we often learn about such events as they are happening.

The role of news media in providing information is vital to a democratic society like ours. In this kind of society, where people vote for their leaders and public opinion helps shape government policy, it is necessary for citizens to make well-informed choices and decisions. In order to make them wisely, citizens need information—information provided, to a great extent, by the news media.

But the news media disseminate more than raw information. They also disseminate ideas. This function, too, is vital to a democratic society. In a sense, the United States owes its very existence to the ability of the news media to disseminate ideas. Without the media, the American Revolution might never have taken place.

Publishers of colonial newspapers (among them Benjamin Franklin) helped to lead the push for American independence from Britain. They were bitterly opposed to the Stamp Acts, Britain's attempts to tax their papers, and they used their newspapers to stir up feeling against British rule. The debate over whether or not to rebel against Britain was conducted largely in the pages of the colonial newspapers, and the Boston Tea Party was planned in a newspaper office. Many American papers called openly for rebellion against the Crown. In the darkest days of the revolution itself, the Patriot press (as it was called) helped to keep up the morale of the revolutionary forces.

Once the revolution succeeded, the American press provided the forum for the great political debate over what form the government of the new country should take. And, after the Constitution was enacted, it wasn't surprising that the very first amendment made to it dealt with the press. Keenly aware of the role the press had played in championing and protecting American freedoms from the power of the colonial government, the founders passed the First Amendment to protect the rights of the press from the new government they were forming. It promised that the new government would "make no law . . . abridging the freedom . . . of the press."

Periodically, some elements of the press have used that freedom to provide a forum for the expression of political ideas—often ideas hostile to the political parties and politicians in power.

The news media actually provide several different forums for ideas. Most publish their own opinions, of course—the opinions of their editors, owners, or publishers—in the form of editorial commentaries. (The term "publish" will be used in this book in its broadest sense, that of "making public." It includes not only print publishing, but broadcasting and other ways of disseminating information as well.) But many of them also publish the views of other journalists, including cartoonists and columnists, who disagree with their editorial positions.

News media of all kinds regularly publish the opinions of political leaders and other public figures in a wide variety of forms, including guest editorials, the texts of public speeches, and quotations from published works and interviews. Many also publish the opinions of ordinary citizens as well, in the form of letters to the editor, man-in-the-street interviews, and the like.

THE SPECIAL IMPACT OF RADIO AND TELEVISION

The introduction of radio and television has added enormously to the pervasiveness of the news media. And these relatively new media have given journalism—and journalists—a new kind of power to influence people.

This influence shows itself most in the world of politics. Television gives the public a greater sense of familiarity with politicians than they ever had before. This is particularly true when it comes to the nation's president, who is inevitably the politician most often seen and heard on television.

This sense of familiarity is a new concept in American history. Before television, relatively few people ever saw a president in the flesh. All most citizens knew of their president was what they heard by word of mouth and, of course, what they read in the newspapers. It is still true that most Americans never get to see a president in person. But thanks to radio and television, both the voice and the face of the current president are instantly recognizable to virtually everyone. Many people feel almost as though they intimately *know* the president. As with other simulated experiences, this intimacy can be misleading. Watching people on television and listening to them on radio is not the same as meeting them and talking to them in person.

However misleading this sense of personal "knowledge" may be, it can have a significant effect on political reality. Some political commentators believe that no candidate can be elected president today unless the people come to feel they know and like him as a person. Some people believe that this sense of intimacy can be even more important than the candidate's policies.

In 1984, for example, a substantial majority of voters voted for Ronald Reagan, even though polls showed that 84 percent of likely voters favored stricter environmental standards, 71 percent favored a nuclear weapons freeze, 61 percent favored affirmative action in employment, and 58 percent favored an Equal Rights Amendment for women—all positions President Reagan was perceived as opposing and his opponent was perceived as supporting.[1] Voters seemed to feel they knew, liked, and trusted the president, so they voted for him even though they disagreed with him on many vital political issues. In most cases, this sense of personal affection was derived entirely from what people had seen and heard in the news media.

Coverage of American successes at the Olympic Games kindles patriotic sentiment.

The ability to broadcast live events allows the electronic media to bring the nation together in times of crisis and celebration alike. It enables people all across the country to share, all at once, in a single national experience.

Some of the experiences, like the explosion of the Challenger in 1986, are tragic. Others, like the centennial celebration for the Statue of Liberty that took place in the same year, are joyful. They, along with many others, have had profound effects on the way we feel about ourselves, both as individuals and as a nation. The extensive coverage of the assassination of President John F. Kennedy in 1963, for example, promoted a widespread feeling of shock and self-examination. The two weeks of coverage of the Los Angeles Olympics in 1984, during which American athletes were shown winning scores of medals, prompted a surge of patriotic feeling throughout the country.

THE IMPORTANCE OF THE PRESS

The power of the media is not absolute, but it is real. There is no good evidence that the press controls public opinion in the United States, in the sense that it tells people what to think. But it does, to a great extent, tell people what to think *about*. Ideas, issues, and events seem to assume greater or lesser importance simply by virtue of their coverage in the press. The more attention they receive in the media, the more important they seem to become to the public at large. The press, then, tends to set the terms of debate on almost every major social and political issue that affects us as a society.

Because so much of the information on which each of us relies in making our political and social decisions comes from the press, and because those individual decisions, added together, determine what our society is, and how it functions—the press helps to determine the very nature and direction of our national political life.[2]

It is because of the pervasiveness and power of the news media that the ethical standards of the journalistic profession should be of vital importance to us all.

2

THE BASIC PRINCIPLES OF JOURNALISM ETHICS

Ethics is concerned with the morality of human behavior, that is, with questions of right and wrong. Whenever we ask whether a given action is good or bad, whether it is morally right or wrong, we are asking an ethical question. Whenever we decide to do something because it is the right thing to do, we are making an ethical decision.

The ethics of a given occupation or profession is the standard of behavior expected of people in that occupation or profession. The ethical standards of some professions are simple, those of others more complex. In some professions, such as medicine, elaborate codes of ethics have been established. In a few professions, people are required to swear to follow the code before being allowed to enter the profession at all. In other professions, the ethical standards are largely unwritten. It is up to each individual to decide what is ethical, based on tradition and common sense.

Still, whether spelled out or not, there are ethical considerations to every job. If a plumber (or a carpenter, or a lawyer, for that matter) charges for more hours than he or she really puts in on a job, he or she is acting unethically. So is the employee who works hard only when the boss is around. So are the car dealer who turns back the odometer of a used car to deceive potential buyers, and the merchant who shortchanges a customer.

On the other hand, when the car dealer is scrupulously honest in describing the condition of a used car to a potential customer, he or she is behaving ethically. So is the merchant who charges a fair price for all merchandise, and the plumber and the employee who put in a fair amount of work for a fair amount of pay.

The ethical considerations in such cases are pretty straightforward, and their effects are relatively limited. What the average plumber, used car dealer, or merchant does affects only a few people. Because of this, their ethical standards are of great interest only to themselves and to their customers.

But there are some professions whose activities affect the entire society in ways that go far beyond the prices paid for particular goods or services. Because these activities are critical to the quality of life of nearly everyone, their ethical standards are of interest to society as a whole. Journalism is one of these vital professions.

CHARGES AGAINST
THE PRESS

Clearly, the press accomplishes much that is good, and useful, for society. Indeed, it would be hard to imagine a modern, democratic society functioning without it. But it is equally clear that the enormous power wielded by the press can be misused.

It is not hard to find criticisms of the American news media. Charges of press abuses of one kind or another are heard from almost every sector of American society, including journalists themselves.

Critics have accused the press of everything from sloppiness and inaccuracy to deliberate dishonesty. The media have been charged with slanting the news (twisting it for purposes of their own). Individual reporters are criticized for being rude and offensive. The press, as a whole, is accused of routinely invading people's privacy and ruining their reputations. Some critics have charged that the American press is unpatriotic; others have accused it of giving away military secrets to the nation's enemies. Still others claim that the press is jingoistic, too blindly pro-American, slanting facts to make the United States look good. On at least one occasion (in 1898) American newspapers were charged with deliberately provoking a pointless war between the United States and Spain in order to boost their own circulations. "War," as one editor said, "sells newspapers."

Most journalists would agree that the press can—and sometimes does—misuse its power. They agree, too, that this misuse is a bad thing, that it should be curtailed. Just how it should be curtailed is the subject of much controversy.

Many nonjournalist critics of the press believe that more legal restraints should be put on what journalists can and cannot do, and on what can and cannot be published. The First Amendment to the Constitution, though, commands that the government play only a limited role, if any, in such decisions. For that reason, among others, most journalists would argue that the admitted abuses by some elements of the press should not be restrained by laws, but only by the ethical standards of journalists themselves.

But what should those ethical standards be?

A FOUNDATION FOR JOURNALISTIC ETHICS

Ethical behavior does not exist in a vacuum. The standards of ethical behavior for any profession have to be set in light of the goals of that profession, and of its duties and obligations toward society.

What are the duties and obligations of the American press in the twentieth century? In 1947, a prestigious independent commission was established to examine that question. Officially entitled the Commission on Freedom of the Press, it was referred to more informally as the Hutchins Commission, after its chairperson Robert M. Hutchins. It reached the following conclusions about the role of the press in modern society: "Today our society needs, first, a truthful, comprehensive, and intelligent account of the day's events in a context which gives them meaning; second, a forum for the exchange of comment and criticism; third, a means of projecting the opinions and attitudes of the groups in the society to one another; fourth, a method of presenting and clarifying the goals and values of the society; and, fifth, a way of reaching every member of the society by the currents of information, thought and feeling which the press supplies."[1]

The commission understood that no single news medium, much less any single news organization, could meet all those needs. But it is in light of those needs that journalists must determine the ethics of their profession.

The American Society of Newspaper Editors (A.S.N.E.) tackled the problem of journalistic ethics in its own way in 1975, adopting a Statement of Principles. Although specifically designed for newspaper journalists, its principles apply equally well to all journalists, in whatever medium they happen to work. Those principles are responsibility, freedom of the press, truth and accuracy, independence, impartiality, and fair play.[2]

Responsibility

In a general sense, responsibility is what ethics is all about. But, in the case of journalism, responsibility for what? And to whom?

Most journalists would say that the press has many responsibilities, among them the duty to uphold each of the other principles spelled out in the A.S.N.E. statement. But they might disagree over which is the deepest, most fundamental responsibility of the American press.

Some would argue that the press owes its first responsibility to some abstract ideal of truth or social justice, others to its own independence and integrity. Still others argue that the real key to the responsibility of the American press lies in the word "American." The press, they say, is given its freedom *by* the nation, and in return it owes its greatest responsibility *to* the nation.

Most journalists, however, would probably agree with the A.S.N.E. statement, which defines the responsibilities of the press in terms of its role in a democratic political system. In this view, the first responsibility of the press is not to the nation, as such, but to the *people* of the nation, to the public. "The primary purpose of gathering and distributing news and opinion," according to the A.S.N.E., "is to serve the general welfare by informing people and enabling them to make judgments on the issues of the time."

This purpose implies a specifically *political* function for the press—the function of watchdog. "The American press," says the A.S.N.E. statement, "was made free not just to inform or just to serve as a forum for debate but also to bring an independent scrutiny to bear on the forces of power in the society, including the conduct of official power at all levels of government."

Freedom of the Press

The Constitution of the United States guarantees that the federal government will not interfere with the freedom of the American press. Most journalists take this guarantee seriously and believe it is their ethical duty to defend freedom of the press at all costs.

There is much controversy about the specific nature and purpose of this freedom. Why should the press be granted special protection from government interference? The Constitution does not say. As seen by the A.S.N.E., however, and by journalists, "Freedom of the press belongs to the people." Any special treatment given the press is granted not as a favor to the press, but as a protection for the public.

Nonetheless, the special treatment given the press places a special obligation on journalists. In guaranteeing a constitutional right to the people, through the press, the A.S.N.E. statement points out, the First Amendment "places . . . a particular responsibility" on the press. "Thus journalism demands of its practitioners not only industry and knowledge but also the pursuit of a standard of integrity proportionate to the journalist's singular obligation." Members of the press "who abuse the power of their professional role for selfish motives or unworthy purposes are faithless to that public trust."

Truth and Accuracy

Truth and accuracy are probably the most commonly understood and widely accepted of all the principles of journalistic ethics. As the A.S.N.E. statement puts it: "Good faith is the foundation of good journalism." After all, people who read something in a newspaper or magazine, hear it on radio, or see it on television, expect it to be both accurate and true.

At first, the phrase "accurate and true" may seem redundant. We tend to assume that what is accurate is inevitably true and that what is true is invariably accurate. But in reality, accuracy and truth are not necessarily the same. A news story can be literally accurate but still untrue, in the sense of being misleading. Bias or lack of context, whether deliberate or not, can distort an otherwise accurate story. A report that a politician had been hissed and booed at a public appearance, for example, might be accurate; but it could still be essentially untrue if it failed to include the fact that the booing had come from only one or two hecklers in the midst of a large and cheering crowd.

Truth and accuracy may be easy concepts to understand, but they are difficult goals to achieve, particularly in the pressure and rush of daily journalism. Reporters often have little time to collect their facts. They are routinely forced to rely on information provided by individuals who are themselves often mistaken, and who sometimes lie. Objective evidence that would clearly prove or disprove a story is rarely available. And after all the information is collected, the reporter is usually given only a limited amount of space in which to explain often complex and difficult-to-understand events. What is more, he or she is forced to write quickly, which contributes to sloppiness and mistakes.

Truth and accuracy are rarely held out as absolute standards to be demanded of working journalists. Instead, they are held up as ideals toward which journalists are expected to strive. The A.S.N.E. statement, for example, does not require that everything published be true and accurate. If that were the standard, very little could be published at all. Rather, the statement directs that, "every effort must be made to assure that the news content is accurate, free from bias and in context, and that all sides are presented fairly." On those occasions when the ideals of truth and accuracy are not met, the statement goes on, "Significant errors of fact, as well as errors of omission, should be corrected promptly and prominently."

Independence

According to the A.S.N.E., the press is obligated to "bring an independent scrutiny to bear on the forces of power in the society." That obligation makes it vital for the press to maintain its independence from those "forces of power."

This independence is vital for two reasons. The first has to do with the need for objectivity. The more things that interfere with a journalist's objectivity, the more difficult it is to fulfill his or her responsibility to give the public accurate and reliable information.

The second has to do with public perception—how the public views the press. The press needs the trust of the public, or at least its respect, if it is to fulfill its necessary functions in our society. A press which is broadly disbelieved cannot be effective as a dispenser of information.

Whether or not the press actually is independent, it will

be unable to win the respect and trust it needs unless the public believes it is independent. It is not enough, then, for the press merely to *be* independent. It has to be *seen to be* independent as well. For this reason, the A.S.N.E. statement declares, it is not sufficient for journalists merely to avoid impropriety. They must avoid any "appearance of impropriety" as well.

Impartiality

Any attempt by journalists to be impartial would seem to be at odds with a long tradition of the American press. That tradition, of taking sides in public controversies, dates back to the Patriot press of the American Revolution, and even before.

Many American newspapers were founded specifically to promote a particular political point of view. Some still carry such partisan names as the Springfield (Mass.) *Union News Republican* and the *Tallahassee Democrat* (Fla.). Even today, many elements of both the print and electronic press make a practice of taking editorial stands on public issues. It would be hard, if not impossible, to find a major daily newspaper without an editorial page. What is more, even the A.S.N.E. statement itself, despite its call for impartiality, defines the distribution of opinion as one of the fundamental functions of the press.

So how can the press be impartial? And why should it be? The answer lies in the fact that impartiality, in this sense of the word, does not mean neutrality. In the words of the A.S.N.E. statement: "To be impartial does not require the press to be unquestioning, or to refrain from editorial expression." What it *does* require is that the press refrain from publishing propaganda in the guise of news; that it restrain itself from slanting news coverage to favor any particular point of view.

There are at least three separate journalistic functions, each requiring a different standard of impartiality. When reporting the facts, journalists consider themselves bound to keep their opinions out of their work altogether. When analyzing and explaining the facts, they consider themselves a little freer to express their opinions, but in a fair and balanced way. And when editorializing, they feel free to express their opinions without any requirement for impartiality at all.

For the A.S.N.E., the ethical key is to label opinion for what it is. Whenever the press takes a side on a public issue, it should do so openly. "Sound practice . . . demands a clear distinction for the reader between news reports and opinion. . . . Articles that contain opinion or personal interpretation should be clearly identified."

In other words, the role of the press in the dissemination of opinion should be kept separate from its news function. Journalists are ethically bound to keep their opinions from influencing their news judgment.

Fair Play

The principle of fair play is one that is honored (though not always practiced) by people in most professions. It is nothing more than dealing with others in an honorable, decent—and therefore ethical—manner.

Just what is or is not fair depends on the particular profession involved. Behavior that is perfectly ethical for members of one profession may be unethical for members of another. This difference can be understood by comparing members of two different professions carrying out a similar activity.

When customers walk into a car dealership, it is understood that a salesperson is going to try to sell them a car, and probably as expensive a car as they can afford. That is the salesperson's job, and he or she is acting according to the ethical standards of that job.

But what is ethical for a salesperson selling a car is not ethical for a doctor. When a patient walks into a doctor's office, he or she is looking for advice and treatment, not a sales pitch. It is unethical, according to the standards of the medical profession, for doctors to attempt to "sell" their patients courses of treatment they don't medically need, simply in order to profit from the fees they would be paid. It would be unfair of a doctor to take advantage of a patient in such a way.

What is fair play for a car salesperson is not necessarily fair play for a doctor. The ethics of certain actions can depend on the relationships involved.

Journalists deal with many people in the course of their work, and in several different relationships. There are the people they use as sources of information, for example, those who are the subjects of their reports, and the public to whom they report, among others. To some extent, the journalist's ethical responsibilities are different toward each of them.

It is up to journalists as individuals, and to news organizations as institutions, to deal fairly with all these different people, in. all these different relationships. The A.S.N.E. statement calls on journalists to: "respect the rights of people involved in the news," even those subjected to criticism by the press; and to give "people publicly accused . . . . the earliest opportunity to respond," as well as to "observe the common standards of decency and stand accountable to the public for the fairness and accuracy of their news reports."

THE NEED FOR INTERPRETATION AND DEBATE

Journalistic organizations are very conscious of the need for professional ethics. Virtually every one of them has a document similar to that put out by the A.S.N.E., designed for its own members or employees. We have used the A.S.N.E. statement here because the basic principles it sets out are among the most widely accepted, and most widely applicable, to be found anywhere.

Nonetheless, like most ethical concepts, these principles are subject to interpretation and debate. Most journalists, along with most critics of the press, would agree on their value as journalistic ideals. But there is controversy, both within the journalistic profession and outside it, over just how these ideals should be applied to specific journalistic practices. What is more, there are times when these principles come into conflict with one another, and choices have to be made between them. Such questions of interpretation and debate, and such choices, are at the heart of the subject of journalistic ethics.

3

CONFLICTS
OF INTEREST

Upholding the independence of the press from corrupting influences is an essential element of ethical journalism. For a journalist not to do so is a violation of professional integrity.

Every failure in the integrity of the press makes it that much more difficult for the press to fulfill its primary responsibility: to "serve the general welfare." Not only do these failures tend to distort the information given to the public, they can destroy the public's confidence in the press. That destruction of confidence, in turn, diminishes the effectiveness of the press. More importantly, it diminishes its usefulness. Only when people feel they can rely on the press's integrity, its basic honesty, will they tend to believe what the press has to tell them. An honest press needs to be believed to be useful. (A dishonest press, of course, should not be believed at all.) It is clear, then, that the integrity of the press and its usefulness to society go hand in hand.

Journalistic integrity begins with the integrity of individual reporters. Their integrity, in turn, depends to a large extent on their ability and willingness to avoid conflicts of interest.

WHAT ARE CONFLICTS
OF INTEREST?

The concept of conflict of interest is central to any discussion of journalistic integrity. One of the most widely accepted of all ethical principles is the Biblical dictum: "A man cannot serve two masters." A conflict of interest arises whenever someone is put in the position of trying to do just that—whenever a person has two goals, or two loyalties, that are in conflict with each other.

For individual journalists, conflicts of interest most often occur when their professional duties conflict with their private interests, that is, when they are called on to cover some issue, individual, or business with which they also have a personal involvement. The term *conflict of interest* is usually used when the private interest involved is economic, but it can also be emotional, or even ideological. The threat to journalistic integrity can be just as real, whatever the private interest involved.

The most blatant of all conflicts of interest is a bribe. An individual might offer money to an editor, for example, in return for publishing a favorable news story or suppressing an unfavorable one. The editor is put in the position of working for two masters with two opposing interests. The first is the news organization, which expects its editors to be objective and to use their independent news judgment. The second is the bribe payer, who wants to dictate what the editor will publish. This is an obvious conflict, which most journalists would recognize as ethically unacceptable and seek to avoid.

A bribe is a direct and obvious attempt to corrupt—a deliberate invitation to a journalist to sell his or her integrity for personal gain. But not all conflicts of interest are so willfull, or even deliberate.

A reporter receives a great deal of information, some of it accurate and some of it not. He or she constantly has to make decisions. Is this piece of information important enough to be included in the story, or can it be left out? Is one source more or less reliable than another? Decisions like these can be influenced by the reporter's personal desires and prejudices, even without the reporter being aware of that influence.

What if a reporter is called on to report about a company in which he or she owns stock? Mightn't the reporter show the company in a better light than it deserves, in order to protect the value of the stock? Or, if the reporter is honest, mightn't he or she be even harder on the company than it deserves, bending over backward to be objective? Either way, the conflict of interest will tend to distort—to corrupt—journalistic judgment.

Precisely because of such dangers, 63 percent of newspaper editors questioned by the A.S.N.E. said it was flatly unethical for a reporter to own stock in a company he or she covers.[1] Twenty-eight percent even considered it a violation of ethics for the husband or wife of a reporter to own such stock. Many responsible journalists, faced with a situation like the one above, would tell their editors about their conflict of interest and ask that the story be assigned to someone else.

Political Conflicts

Not all conflicts of interest involve money. A reporter who contributes time as a volunteer speechwriter for a political candidate would have a conflict of interest if asked to report on the candidate's campaign—or on the campaign of the candidate's opponent.

Some of the problems that can arise from this kind of conflict were demonstrated in 1980. In that year's presidential campaign, the political columnist George Will helped Ronald Reagan prepare himself for a televised debate with the then president, Jimmy Carter. After the debate, Will appeared on television himself, praising Reagan's performance without mentioning his own part in it. When his connection to the debate was eventually revealed, Will defended himself on the grounds that he was a political *commentator*, not a reporter. Besides, everyone already knew he was a Reagan supporter. There was no need, he felt, for him to spell out exactly what he had done. But another Washington journalist, James McCartney, had a different point of view. Will, he complained, "has made every reporter in Washington look like he may be in the bag."[2]

A reporter asked to cover a possible scandal involving an old personal friend would have a conflict of interest between the natural personal desire to protect a friend and the professional responsibility to uncover the truth, however damaging that truth might be. A reporter asked to cover the affairs of a personal enemy would have a similar ethical problem, only in reverse.

Conflicts of interest don't necessarily spring from corrupt motives. Journalists don't have to be personally dishonest or lacking in moral character to be influenced by them. But all conflicts of interest are corrupting, because they interfere with the objectivity of journalists' perceptions, and the independence of their judgment. (Consider how hard it would be for a male reporter on the school paper to be objective covering an election for prom queen or class president if his girlfriend were one of the candidates.)

Some journalists feel that they won't be affected by a particular conflict of interest, so they try to ignore it, to carry on with their job as though it didn't exist. Others think this is self-deception. Although they don't deny that it might be possible to report objectively despite a particular conflict of interest, they argue that it is impossible for a reporter to be sure that he or she is doing so. It is precisely because one cannot be sure whether a conflict of interest *is* distorting one's judgment that conflicts are so dangerous.

Curbing Conflicts

Some news organizations have written codes of ethics to which reporters and editors can refer when they're not sure if a given action would place them in a conflict of interest. Others leave it up to the judgments of the individual reporters and their superiors to recognize and correct any conflicts. But all responsible news organizations are concerned about the problem, and most do their best to cut down on potential conflicts of interest by placing restrictions on their employees.

Personal friendships are, of course, hard to regulate, but journalists are generally discouraged from associating privately with the people they cover. If assigned to cover a story involving a personal friend, enemy, or business associate, a reporter is expected to reveal the relationship. Someone else is usually given the responsibility of determining whether that relationship constitutes a sufficient conflict of interest for the reporter to be removed from the story.

Some news organizations require their employees to get permission before they take any kind of outside employment whatsoever, even employment that has nothing to do with their jobs as journalists. Most, if not all, major news organizations forbid employees to hold any outside employment that might cause a conflict of interest (or even an appearance of such a conflict) with their duties as journalists. Because of the special relationship between the press and the government, restrictions on outside employment often include any work, paid or unpaid, for any branch of local, state, or federal government. Some news organizations even forbid work for any entity significantly funded by the government.

Some are even stricter, forbidding their employees to work for any outside employer who does business with their organization, even when that business is totally unrelated to the job the journalist performs. (Some, although not all, make an exception for volunteer work done for a charity.) Some carry the prohibition one step further. They forbid employees to moonlight for public relations agencies that handle accounts of companies who place advertisements with them, even when the journalists' work has nothing to do with those particular accounts.

In order to keep reporters from becoming personally

indebted to news sources, some news organizations have firm policies forbidding their employees from accepting gifts or other favors from any current or potential news sources. Some even extend this prohibition to include such minor items as food or drink. Not all are that strict, however. Several permit specified small exceptions, such as business-related meals, or tickets for events the journalist is scheduled to review. But virtually all news organizations recognize the potential ethical problems inherent in journalists accepting even small gifts from people or organizations likely to turn up in the news.

Most news organizations permit their employees to own stock in public corporations and even to own their own businesses, as long as they don't cover any news involving companies they own. Some, however, fear the appearance of conflict of interest, not so much for the individual reporter, but for the organization itself. They worry that others, looking at the situation from outside, may *think* that the reporter's connection with the business is affecting the way news about the business is handled. As a result, they forbid ownership in any business that either advertises with the journalist's organization or that seeks free publicity from it. Most, however, would not go so far. As long as the reporter's work is not related to his or her outside business interests, they do not object to them.

THE POWER
OF ADVERTISERS

Traditionally, one of the greatest threats to the integrity of American journalism has been the influence of advertisers.

Most newspapers, magazines, and radio and television networks and stations depend on the income they derive from advertisers. That fact gives the advertisers a certain amount of influence over them. Just how great that influence is, and how directly it affects the news that they publish, is unclear.

Almost certainly such influence is less than it used to be. The news columns of most nineteenth- and early-twentieth-century papers were filled with favorable references to the local businesses that advertised in them. In the early days of radio and television, journalists had to be approved by the sponsors of the news programs on which they would be featured. There are indications that, to some extent at least, the content of the news had to be approved as well. In the days before cigarette advertising was banned from television, for example, cigarette companies were heavy advertisers on network news shows; few stories about the dangers of cigarette smoking appeared on those shows.

Today, most major organizations have policies requiring that their news and advertising departments be kept separate. Theoretically, at least, the two are to have no effect on each other. In this way, the independence of the news department is supposed to be assured.

Still, most observers who have studied the media believe that a great deal of influence still exists. In some small towns and rural areas, there is no question. The local papers are almost as filled with puffery for local advertisers as they were a century ago.[3]

Even in major metropolitan areas, many newspapers regularly run articles extolling the virtues of local businesses and the people who run them. In addition, they often feature stories and editorials boosting civic projects and activities sponsored by those businesses. (Much the same is true of local radio and television stations.)

Some press critics believe that whole sections of many newspapers may only exist *because* of advertisers. Why, they ask, do so many newspapers have a weekly travel section in their Sunday editions? The answer, they suggest, is economic rather than journalistic. It is the heavy amount of advertising purchased in those sections by airlines and tourist agencies.

In March 1986, the prestigious *New York Times* ran a color supplement to its weekly *The New York Times Magazine* called *Men's Fashions of the Times.* In between full-page ads for products like Clinique Skin Supplies for Men and Calvin Klein blue jeans were articles with titles like "How to Dress for Summer" and "The California Look." These articles were illustrated with full-color photos of men's fashions, each item described in a caption telling who designed the product, where it could be bought, and how much was being charged for it. (This sort of description is standard in many fashion articles.) It might be argued that those articles merely filled an interest among *Times* readers about the latest trends in men's fashions. But it could also be argued that there was little, if any, difference between the articles and the advertisements, and that the former would never have been published if not for the latter.

CONTROVERSIES

Even experienced journalists don't always agree on just what is a conflict of interest and what isn't. And not all conflicts of interest are equally serious.

Some practices are clearly unethical in the eyes of most journalists. When asked by the A.S.N.E., for example, fully 99 percent of 226 newspaper editors polled agreed that the use of unpublished information for personal financial gain was unethical. Seventy-one percent said they would suspend, or even fire, a reporter for doing so. An equally overwhelming 99 percent frowned on the practice of selling tickets to events which had been given to the paper for the use of critics or sportswriters. But only 31 percent said they would suspend or fire a reporter caught doing so. (Some news organizations refuse to accept free tickets at all.)

The difference in the seriousness of the above cases is twofold. First, the use of unpublished information is likely to involve a larger sum of money. Knowledge that could affect the price of a stock, for example, might result in an unethical profit of tens of thousands of dollars. A few tickets, on the other hand, even to a major sporting event, would probably involve no more than a few hundred dollars at the most.

Second, and perhaps more importantly, the two cases involve violations of two very different kinds of trust. The sale of free tickets is essentially a violation of the trust between the journalist and his or her employer. A ticket given for a use which would ultimately benefit the paper (the appearance of a story on the event) is used for the private profit of an employee instead. The first situation, on the other hand, involves a violation of the trust between the journalist and the *public.* Information which could benefit a reporter financially could benefit members of the public as well. It is the reporter's job to provide that information to the public. By withholding it from them, and using it for personal gain instead, the reporter has, in a sense, cheated the public. Considering the journalist's responsibility to serve the public, many editors regard that as a much more serious offense than cheating an employer.

Even the use of information that *is* shared with the public can be a problem. A reporter for the *Wall Street Journal* named R. Foster Winans was fired in 1986 for giving a friend business information he knew would be published in the *Journal* the next day. The ethical problem here involved timing. Winans and his friend assumed the information would make people want to buy stock in certain companies. The friend used the information to buy stock *before* the public was given the information in the paper. When the stock price went up after the news was published, the friend would be able to sell the stock for a profit.[4]

The scheme was not only journalistically unethical, it was illegal. Courts found that it violated federal laws against using nonpublic "inside" information to make money from stocks.

Editors' attitudes toward some practices depend heavily on specific circumstances. Political campaign contributions by reporters are frowned upon by most editors. But they are much more widely condemned when they are made to candidates on the reporter's beat than when they are made to others. Ninety-three percent of the polled editors considered such contributions unethical when given to a candidate the reporter covered regularly, and 29 percent would actually suspend or even fire a reporter for making them. Only 66 percent would object to contributions made to a candidate not on the reporter's beat, however, and a mere 7 percent would do more than reprimand the reporter involved.

Motivation can make a difference as well. Seventy-five percent of the editors felt that it was wrong for a reporter to write ad copy for an outside business, even when that business was not on the reporter's beat. But only 59 percent considered it unethical for a reporter to write similar copy for nonprofit organizations.

Some editors hold different categories of journalists to different ethical standards. Eighty-six percent would question the ethics of a reporter who collected a fee for speaking to a group on his or her beat, but only 67 percent would object to a photographer doing freelance work under similar circumstances.

As we have seen, whether a specific situation constitutes a conflict of interest is sometimes open to question. But few, if any, journalists would deny that real conflicts of interest do exist. The challenge they present to the integrity of individual reporters is a threat to the integrity of journalism itself.

4

RELATIONSHIPS WITH SOURCES

One of a reporter's main jobs is dealing with sources, people who supply information. There are many different kinds of sources: official sources, representatives of government or private agencies whose job is to direct the flow of information to the press, as well as private citizens who give information to the press for reasons of their own. Some volunteer their information, others have to be sought out and persuaded to talk to the press. Some are people the reporter has never met before and will never meet again. Others are people he or she knows well.

Reporters often have on-going relationships with sources, people they see and talk to often, who provide them with information on a more or less regular basis. This is especially true of sources on a reporter's regular beat. A beat is a particular institution or area of interest which a reporter covers on an on-going basis. Examples of beats might include the local police force, a particular industry, or the state legislature.

These continuing relationships can be especially helpful to reporters on certain kinds of beats, such as the local police or the state legislature. Because institutions like these have specific, limited memberships, and because so much of their business is conducted behind closed doors, "inside" information is often particularly important to the reporters who cover them. Any reporter who can establish an on-going, friendly relationship with a member of the police force, or a key state legislator, is likely to get more (and more reliable) information about those organizations than the average reporter. Consequently, many reporters who regularly cover those beats do their best to cultivate relationships with people "in the know."

These relationships can present reporters with serious ethical problems. A reporter who regularly meets with a public figure, for example, discussing family and other private matters in order to draw the person out, may cross the line between being a disinterested reporter and being a friend. The reporter is still obliged to cover that public figure objectively, but it is hard for anyone to be objective about a friend.

Even when friendship is not involved, there is a tendency on the part of reporters who associate extensively with their sources to identify themselves with them, and to lose objectivity. A police reporter, for example, who spends a great deal of time with police officers—eating with them, drinking with them, visiting their homes, and even accompanying them on patrol—can begin to start thinking and feeling like a police officer. When that happens, it becomes more difficult, if not impossible, for the journalist to report objectively (or even fairly) on police matters. Asked to report on allegations of police brutality made by a citizen against police officers, for example, a police reporter may tend to side with the police. He or she may either assume that the citizen is lying about being beaten by the police, or that even if the incident occurred the police officers were justified in what they did.

Problems like these can occur on any beat, and not just with individual sources, but with whole institutions. When the space shuttle Challenger blew up shortly after liftoff in 1986, most Americans were not only saddened by the event, they were shocked. They had no reason to assume from what they had heard in the media that anything like that could ever happen. The media had given little, if any, indication of serious safety problems within the manned space program. Many observers (including many journalists themselves) concluded that there had been a tendency among the reporters covering the National Aeronautics and Space Administration (NASA) to identify with the space program—to become boosters for it, praise its accomplishments, and overlook or underreport its problems. "For 30 years," two observers wrote, journalists "had covered the space program as an awesome and pioneering venture, a source of national prestige. . . . Virtually all news about the shuttle came directly from NASA officials and its public relations staff through a well-rehearsed system of press releases and news briefings." The result had been an "uncritical style" of reporting that finally backfired, "damaging both the credibility of the press and the public's trust in American technological enterprise."[1]

Close relationships of all kinds, whether with people or institutions, present journalists with an ethical dilemma. On the one hand, such relationships are a useful means of obtaining information—information which, after all, it is their duty to obtain and publish. On the other hand, the same relationships are likely to taint the news judgment of reporters, at the very least, and perhaps even to strain their integrity.

Journalists are divided on the ethics of such relationships. Only 15 percent of the editors responding to the A.S.N.E. survey, for example, felt it was clearly unethical for a reporter to socialize with an individual he or she wrote about often, but 49 percent said they discouraged their reporters from doing so. Some apparently believed that the journalistic benefits to be gained from those relationships outweighed the dangers, while others believed the opposite.

PAYING FOR
INFORMATION

Reporters' relations with their sources are usually reciprocal. That is, the transmission of information involves a kind of transaction. The source expects something in return for the information, a kind of price to be paid for it. Often, that price is nothing more than publication of the information. The source provides the information for the specific purpose of publicizing it, getting it out to the public. In this case (assuming the information is reliable), the transaction presents no ethical problem for the reporter. It is the reporter's job to get the information out to the public. The reporter's interest and the source's price are one and the same.

Sometimes, however, the source will demand a different kind of price for his or her information, whether in money or in some other commodity. Such demands can present the reporter with serious ethical questions.

Few legitimate news organizations like the idea of paying money for news stories. Many have strict policies against doing so. Not all the reasons newspeople dislike paying for information have to do with ethics. Some news organizations, for example, refuse to ·pay because they fear getting into a bidding war with their competitors, a war in which the source could play each against the others, trying to get the best price for their information.

Others argue that paying sources distorts the journalistic process in at least two important ways. Placing an economic value on a news story affects both the reliability of the source and the news judgment of the journalist involved. It gives potential sources a financial incentive to sensationalize their information—to try to make it more saleable by exaggeration, if not to make it up in the first place. At the same time, it tends to distort the journalist's news judgment. Having made a financial commitment to the source, and to the story, the journalist is more likely to *want* to believe in the story. Few reporters would look forward to informing their editors that they spent a large amount of their employers' money on a story that turned out to be either untrue or insignificant. Consequently, many journalists simply refuse to consider paying for information under any circumstances.

Other journalists, however, will consider paying if the information is important—and exclusive—enough. They believe that their obligation to collect and publish the news is more important than their scruples about paying for it.

The payments demanded by sources can vary widely, from a free meal to the $600,000 (plus a share of the profits) reportedly paid to ex-President Richard Nixon for a series of television interviews with David Frost in 1977. The fee was large, but, critics argued, the actual news value of the interviews turned out to be small.[2]

Some sources will only provide information in return for other information held by the reporter. But 74 percent of editors questioned said that giving nonpublic information to an "interested party" was a violation of professional ethics. The hypothetical situation presented to the editors did not stipulate that the information was given in return for other, publishable information, however. If it had, the percentage of editors disapproving the practice might have been smaller, because there would have been an offsetting journalistic reason for doing it.

Sometimes a source will agree to provide information only in return for the reporter's agreement *not* to publish certain other information which the reporter already has. This presents the journalist with an even less appealing ethical choice.

It is probably true, however, that for most journalists, the ethics of paying for information—whether in information, money, or some other commodity—depends on the details of the transaction. When journalists believe that they, and the public, are getting more than they are giving up, most will consider the transaction ethically justified.

ANONYMOUS SOURCES

Sometimes sources don't want the public—or particular members of the public—to know they gave information to the press. Those whose information involves scandalous matters may want to avoid the notoriety that might attach to them if their connection to the story were known. Others, whose information would be harmful to other people or organizations, are afraid of possible retaliation if their identities were made public. Still others, with information about criminal matters, might be worried about trouble with the police. For such reasons, many potential sources will not talk to the press at all unless they are assured of anonymity.

Just how important this kind of confidentiality can be was demonstrated by *Washington Post* reporters Bob Woodward and Carl Bernstein in their coverage of the Watergate scandal. Many of the sources they used for their reports—including the most important source of all, whom they referred to only as "Deep Throat"—insisted on confidentiality before they would talk. Many people believe that some of the most important facts of the scandal would never have come out if it were not for the willingness of the *Post* to grant that confidentiality.[3]

In general, however, journalists would prefer to publish the identity of their sources. Knowing the source can help the public judge the reliability of the information. Journalists are sometimes obliged to publish information, often obtained from one or two sources, that cannot be verified beyond doubt. Sometimes it cannot be verified at all. How can the public decide whether or not to believe the report, unless they know the source of the information?

Sources who provide information that reflects positively on themselves, or negatively on their enemies, for example, may be less believable than those whose information reflects badly on themselves. Or a given source may be in an especially good (or bad) position to know something. Information about the financial affairs of a company might be considered more reliable if obtained from the treasurer of the company, for example, than if it came from someone who worked for a competitor. Word of what was discussed by a jury in a jury room would be more authoritative if it came from the foreman of the jury than if it came from someone who claimed to have listened to the jury's deliberations through a window. In cases like these, knowing the source would help the public enormously in deciding how much weight to give the information in their own minds.

There are still other problems with anonymous sources. For one thing, they are difficult to refute. A person attacked in the press has two main arguments to advance in his or her defense: first, that the allegations are demonstrably untrue; second, that the source of the allegations is unreliable. The first course is not always practical, even when the allegations are false. It is often impossible to "prove" a negative. And, if the source of the allegations is allowed to remain anonymous, the second line of defense is gone. If dishonest people can give information to the press with the assurance that no one will ever find out their identities, they will be freer to lie, and harder to catch if they do.

For the press, protecting the identity of a source can mean withholding more from the public than just the source's name. It can mean withholding the source's *purpose* as well. Take the case of damaging information about a political candidate, provided by that candidate's opponent. The damaging information is news, and of legitimate interest to the voters. The fact that the candidate's opponent was willing to provide that information to the press, and only in secret, is of legitimate interest to the voters as well.

In this kind of situation, a reporter faces a serious dilemma. To publish the information, while allowing the source to remain anonymous, is in effect to help one candidate, harm another, and conceal information from the public as well. Not to publish is to also withhold information from the public, and that, in effect, helps the *other* candidate. If journalists publish the information *and* reveal the identity of the source, they may not be withholding anything from the public, but they are hurting their own ability to gather information in the future. Knowing that the press has betrayed the trust of one source, other potential sources may be reluctant to talk to the press at all.

Although some journalists refuse to deal with anonymous sources, most do not. They are willing to concede that the information they will receive is more valuable than the fact of the source's identity. If the price for revealing an important fact to the public is concealing the source of that fact, they are willing to pay it.

Even among news organizations that use anonymous sources, however, the practice is often discouraged. Some news organizations place restrictions on *when* they will allow a source to remain anonymous, refusing, for example, to grant confidentiality to a source unless disclosure would endanger the source's security. Even then, exceptions are sometimes made when political information is involved.

Leaks

The leak is a particular kind of anonymous information, usually given to the press by someone in government. The term comes from the assumption that the government wants to keep the information secret, but that it "leaks" out anyway. But, in fact, the specific source of a leak wants it to be published.

Government officials leak information for a variety of reasons. Sometimes the reasons are personal—politicians leak information to further their own careers or to injure the careers of their rivals. One candidate for an important position in a government agency, for example, might leak information which will be damaging to the reputation of another.

Sometimes, however, information is leaked for what might be called a public purpose. An official who believes the government is about to make a bad mistake might leak word of the government's plans. By making the proposed action public, he or she hopes to provoke enough public pressure to head it off.

The leak raises some special ethical problems for the journalist. Critics of the practice believe that officials who leak information are being disloyal, if not to the government itself, at least to their particular departments and to their colleagues. For a reporter to use leaked information may be, to some extent, to participate in that betrayal.

Worst of all, they argue, leaks undermine the ability of government to function effectively. Politicians and government workers who cannot rely on one another to keep information confidential will not communicate openly and honestly with each other. Perhaps even more importantly, according to Secretary of State George Shultz, leaks are undermining our relations with other countries. Even our friends, he claims, are "becoming increasingly reluctant to deal with us," and even, in some cases, to communicate with us. They fear that any communication with the United States government, no matter how secret, will be leaked and quickly made public.[4]

To the extent that these criticisms are valid some journalists see a conflict betweeen their ethical duty as journalists and their ethical duty as citizens.

But leaks are two-edged swords. They can be used as effectively to support official government policy as to undermine it.

Presidential administrations and government agencies are as willing as anyone else to use leaks to float trial balloons or discredit opponents. Many working reporters have received leaks from the same high government officials who later made outraged public statements condemning the leak and vowing to punish the leaker.

Some journalists accept such semi-official leaks with gratitude. Others do not. There are journalists who disapprove of leaks every bit as strongly as any government official does, but for very different reasons. They feel uncomfortable about allowing themselves to become a part of such a process. They feel that by accepting leaked information they are, in effect, letting the press be used as a tool of the government: a handy, if indirect, weapon for the government to use to help its friends, attack its enemies, or test the waters of public opinion. That, they argue, is a violation of the press' duty to remain independent. How can the press act as a watchdog over the government when it is cooperating with that government, keeping or revealing its secrets, more or less on order?

PROTECTING THE SOURCE

Most journalists, even those who generally disapprove of anonymous sources, believe that once a journalist has pledged to keep the identity of a source secret, he or she must keep the promise. While warning that pledges of confidentiality must not be given "lightly," the A.S.N.E. Statement of Principles affirms that such pledges, once given, "must be honored at all costs." The *Washington Post*'s code of standards and ethics guarantees that when "we agree to protect a source's identity, that identity will not be made known to anyone outside the *Post*."[5] (Many news organizations will allow the use of anonymous sources only after the reporter has revealed the source's true identity to the editor or publisher or both, so that the superior involved can judge the source's reliability for themselves.)

Some news organizations make exceptions. The Code of Professional Standards of the Chicago *Sun-Times* and *Daily News* states that those papers "commit themselves to protect and defend the identity of confidential news sources," but that this commitment extends only to those sources who provide "information considered valid for publication."[6]

For some newspeople, the obligation to protect a source stops at the point of legal compulsion. That is, if the government (or even a party to a lawsuit) goes to court and receives a court order requiring them to reveal the source of specific information, they will do so. Some obey the order because they are reluctant to go to jail or face the fines that may result from a refusal to obey the court. Others see it as a conflict of ethical standards. They feel that their ethical duty as citizens to obey the legal order of a court comes before their ethical duty as journalists to protect their source.

Not all feel this way, however, and a number of journalists have suffered for their refusal to name a source. Annette Buchanan, the editor of a student newspaper, was fined for refusing to give a grand jury the names of fellow students who had told her about drug use on the campus of the University of Oregon, for instance. Several journalists have actually gone to jail in order to protect sources. These include not only reporters like John F. Lawrence, a bureau chief of the *Los Angeles Times*, but editors and other journalists as well. In at least one case, a television station manager (Edwin A. Goodman of station WBAI in New York) went to jail for refusing to turn over tape recordings which might have identified sources for a report on a prison riot.[7]

Several states have attempted to solve this ethical dilemma for journalists by passing what are known as "shield laws." These give reporters the legal right to refuse to name their sources under most circumstances. Most states, however, do not have such laws. And even in those that do, the shields do not always prove effective. The Supreme Court of the United States ruled in 1972 that "newsmen are not exempt from the normal duty of appearing before a grand jury and answering questions relevant to a criminal investigation. . . . "[8]

The whole issue of anonymous sources—if and when to use them, and just how far to go in protecting them— remains one of the most controversial in journalism today.

5

BEING USED

Many people try to use the press for their own purposes, and those purposes are often political. In this chapter and the next, we will discuss some of the ways that politically motivated individuals and groups, including the government itself, attempt to use the press.

Both politicians and journalists have a vital interest in information. But their interests are very different. The journalist's interest is in *disseminating* information; the politician's interest, in *controlling* it. The journalist wants to make sure that as much information as possible gets to the public. The politician wants to make sure that as much good information (that is, favorable to the politician) gets to the public as possible, and that as much bad information (that is, unfavorable) remains hidden.

Despite this fundamental difference, journalists and politicians need one another. Journalists need politicians for the information they can provide, while politicians need journalists for the (favorable) publicity they can provide. The result of this mutual need is an ongoing, uneasy, and definitely only partial alliance. In that alliance, each side tries to use the other as much as possible without being used too much in return. Some journalists live fairly comfortably with this alliance. Others distrust and fear it. They worry that it allows politicians, both inside and outside of government, far too much influence over what the press is able to reveal to the public.

ON THE RECORD

Politicians and journalists are accustomed to dealing with—and using—each other. They have been doing it for a long time. Over the years, they have worked out a series of unstated ground rules under which information can be transmitted from politicians to the press and finally to the public at large. These ground rules are well understood by both sides.

Most information is transmitted "on the record," which simply means that the reporter is free to use the information any way he or she wants and can identify the source by name. There are two subcategories of on-the-record information, however: that which can be quoted directly, and that which can only be quoted indirectly. In the first case, statements can be printed with quotation marks around them, or, if recorded, broadcast directly. In the second, they can only be summarized, or used without quotation marks.

Journalists usually prefer to get information on the record when possible. The main reason for this preference is philosophical: it is the duty of the press to reveal information, not to conceal it, and the identity of a source is a piece of information. To that extent, not to reveal a source goes against the grain of the profession. But, as we have seen in the previous chapter, reporters are sometimes willing to take information to be used anonymously as well.

Sometimes information is given "on background." In this case, the source will only be referred to indirectly, often by category: "an Administration source," or "a high-ranking official," or simply "a reliable source." Although references like these give clues to the source of the information, the clues are always broad enough to cover a

large number of possible indentities, and they are some-times obscure. Members of the public may assume, when they see this kind of attribution, that the reporter is inflat-ing the importance of the source. A minor official is being called "a key member of the department," for example, or a congressperson's secretary a "congressional source." It's probably true that some reporters have used attribu-tions in that way, to make their information seem more authoritative than it is. But just as often an anonymous attribution has the opposite effect. Terms like "White House official," for example, have been used to describe the president himself.[1]

As a general rule, reporters try to describe their source's position as accurately as possible without reveal-ing his or her actual identity. That effort is always a matter of judgment. (It is not always a matter of the *reporter's* judgment, however. The way in which a source will be described is sometimes negotiated between the reporter and the source.)

Many politicians seem to feel comfortable talking on background and use the practice often. It is a handy way to get one's views reflected in the press. It is also useful for floating trial balloons—testing public reaction to a possible course of action before actually implementing it. For the reporter, trial balloons present a special ethical problem all their own. In publishing them, the press is reporting some-thing that only *might* be true; and in doing so, it is helping to determine whether or not it *will* come true. In effect, the press has become a participant in a process launched by the government (or a politician) in its own interests.

In the cases of both "on the record" and "on back-ground" information, it is given on the understanding that it can be used, if only under certain conditions. Journalists can argue that the ethical compromise involved in such arrangements is justified to get the information out. But when information is given on "deep background" or "off the record," the ethical problem is much greater. Such information is given on the understanding that it will not be

"The Administration Does Not Feel Reporters
Have A Right To Protect Their Source Of Information. . . .
. . . . But Don't Quote Me. This Is Strictly Off The Record."

used at all. Deep background is, in effect, a way for a politician to enlist the help of the press in keeping a secret from the public.

Why, it might be asked, would a politician (or anyone else) want to talk to the press off the record? Why give information to journalists at all if you don't want it to be made public? It is usually done for one of three reasons: to justify specific actions in the eyes of the press, to head off uninformed speculation, or simply to safeguard a secret.

A government intelligence agency, for example, might be upset by press criticisms of intelligence operations that had failed. In order to head off further attacks, the agency might inform reporters off the record about the success of certain other clandestine (or secret) activities that could not be admitted publicly. In this way, even though the information could not be used directly to improve the agency's standing with the public, it might convince the press to mute its criticism.

A politician might be willing to admit to certain things about his or her private life off the record in order to keep members of the press from publishing rumors. A political candidate who had canceled several public appearances without explanation, for example, might confess to having serious family problems in order to prevent the press from speculating on other possible reasons for the seemingly erratic behavior.

In time of war, the military might inform reporters, off the record, of future operations. The intention would be to ensure that the journalists don't discover the plans in other ways and feel free to publish them; or unwittingly publish other information, of troop movements, for instance, which might inadvertently give away the plans to an enemy.

In order to accept information off the record, or even on simple background, a reporter has to make a deal with the source—a deal that requires the reporter to withhold information from the public as a condition of receiving the information at all.

Those journalists who routinely accept information under these conditions argue that they have to do so in order to get other information to give the public. After all, politicians with inside information are not obliged to reveal it to the press. If they cannot rely on journalists to keep confidences, the politicians will simply become more secretive about everything. In the end, the result will be that less and less information will reach the public.

Other journalists disagree. Arrangements like these, they say, don't just surrender the independence that is vital to an effective press, they violate the basic function of journalism itself—to provide information to the public.

What is important is not what the press knows. It is what the public knows. The press is merely a conduit for information, a vehicle by which information passes to the public. For this reason, it is at least arguably unethical for a reporter to withhold any information from the public, under any circumstances.

Most journalists would probably not go so far. They would argue that there can be valid reasons to withhold specific information: the need to protect military secrets from an enemy, for example, or to avoid endangering hostages. In cases like these, they argue, the journalist's responsibility as an American, or even as a human being, can override his or her professional responsibility as a journalist. Some press independence may have to be surrendered for the greater good of protecting the national interest or protecting human lives.

But, say some critics, that reasoning is valid only in the most exceptional circumstances. It can't be applied to the routine arrangements made between politicians and the press. What right, they ask, do journalists—whose duty is to *inform* the public—have to keep information *from* the public? How do such deals with politicians serve the best interest of the public? Or even of the press? Don't they really serve only the best interests of the politicians themselves? And aren't those interests often both self-serving

The news media invariably pick up on powerful visual messages such as this poster held by an anti-abortion demonstrator.

and disreputable? Reporters and news organizations, they argue, shouldn't accept any restrictions on how they will use the information they receive other than those of their own journalistic and ethical standards.

MEDIA EVENTS

One of the main reasons people try to manipulate the press is to obtain publicity, whether for themselves or for a cause they support. Both individuals and groups have found that one way to achieve that goal is to manufacture · a newsworthy event.

The principle is simple. If an event is newsworthy enough—if it is something the public either needs to know or would be greatly interested in knowing—the press will be bound to cover it. Simply by staging such an event, virtually any person or group can assure themselves of attention in the press.

Daredevils make use of this principle when they scale skyscrapers in order to publicize their activities. Strikers make use of it when they block the entrance to a factory to draw attention to their grievances. Farmers, angry at the low prices they receive for their dairy products, make use of it when they dump truckloads of milk in protest.

Publicity may be only one reason for these events. Strikers picketing a plant may also hope to discourage other workers from entering, and thus to put pressure on the owners, for example. But publicity is often an important motive, and sometimes the main one. In any case, few people stage such events without notifying the news media in advance.

Many of the groups that stage events like these are trying to influence public events in some way. Civil rights advocates in the 1950s and '60s, for example, held marches and sit-ins in the south in order to force an end to legal segregation. It worked. Dramatic newspaper photos of white policemen clubbing protestors' heads, and television footage of segregationist sheriffs siccing attack dogs on women and children, aroused sympathy for the cause of desegregation throughout the country. Today, anti-abortion activists picket abortion clinics and thrust glass jars containing aborted human fetuses in front of television cameras, hoping to arouse public indignation—and ultimately political action—against the practice.

In a very different kind of staged event, each of the major political parties holds a national convention every four years and invites the television networks to cover it live. It is far from coincidence that major speeches and appearances by the party's presidential candidates are usually scheduled to occur during prime TV viewing time.

The above are called media events. That is, they are designed to attract as much coverage from the news media as possible, and particularly from television. If the media were not to cover events like these, most would either not take place at all or would be very different in nature.

These events have something else in common, something that troubles many serious journalists. They turn the news media into propagandists for whatever cause the stagers of the events are trying to promote. This doesn't necessarily occur because of the *way* in which the media cover such events. It occurs by virtue of the fact that the media covers them at all.

COVERING TERRORISM

The journalists' dilemma is particularly troubling when it comes to those media events commonly referred to as terrorism. All over the world, relatively small groups of terrorists repeatedly win international attention for their causes by kidnapping foreign citizens, exploding car bombs on crowded city streets, hijacking airplanes, or by committing any one of a number of other terrorist acts.

Inevitably, such dramatic and usually bloody activities receive widespread coverage in the press. Pictures of the resulting death and destruction become instantly familiar around the world. Speculation about the terrorists appears in all the media.

In the case of ongoing terrorist acts like hijackings, or the kidnapping of American citizens abroad, news coverage can be intense. Developments are carried daily above the fold on the front pages of newspapers across the country. The television networks lead off their nightly news shows with the story, and even interrupt their entertainment schedules with bulletins.

Most terrorists are working toward some dramatic political change—the establishment of a Palestinian homeland in the Middle East, the independence of Northern Ireland from Britain, or the independence of the Basque Province from Spain, for example—and fear that their cause is in danger of being overlooked by the major powers of the world. Repeated acts of international violence are one way to keep the world's attention. By giving them that attention, some critics of the press believe, the press encourages terrorism. It becomes a kind of accomplice in the terrorists' bloody acts.

Some critics go so far as to suggest that the press should not cover terrorist acts at all. Others say the press should report them, but only with the simplest possible announcement: what happened, where, and when. The story should appear once, when the act occurs, and then be ignored. No attention at all should be given to the identity of the terrorists, their causes, or the demands that they make.

Since terrorists commit their acts largely to obtain attention in the press, critics argue, withdrawing that attention might stop the acts altogether, or at least reduce their number. Even if the acts were not stopped or lessened, journalists would at least be freed of what some critics see as their moral complicity in the terrorists' murderous activities.

Despite some uneasiness about their role, most journalists reject such suggestions. Hijackings, car bombs, and the like are news. They are real, they happen, and

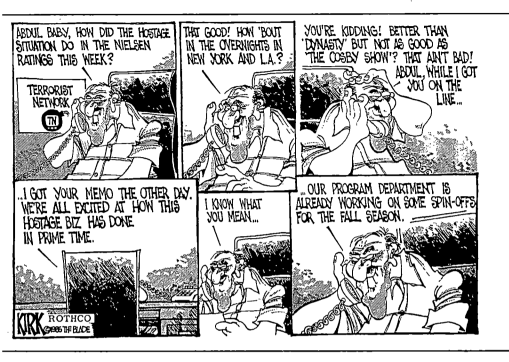

they have important consequences. The press, most journalists feel, has the duty to inform the public about such
events, no matter how distasteful that duty may sometimes be.

In addition to the fact that the public is enormously
interested in terrorist events, defenders of press coverage
point out that the press is far from the only institution in
American society that helps promote interest in terrorism.
The government itself regularly draws attention to it by
publicly responding to it in all sorts of ways, from verbally
condemning some terrorist acts to sending American
planes to bomb Libyan cities in retaliation for others. Even
if the American press could be asked to ignore the acts of
terrorists, it could hardly be expected to ignore the actions
its own government takes against them.

As to the suggestion that the press should refrain from revealing the identities of the terrorists, or describing the causes they represent and the demands they make, most journalists feel that to do so would be irresponsible. Identity and motive are key elements in the story of any criminal activity, and even more so when that activity has political motives and consequences. It is only in the light of political motives and events that terrorism can be understood at all.

Terrorism is clearly news in the world today. So long as it is, journalists will feel they must give it a great deal of attention, however uncomfortable some may feel about doing so. And many of them *do* feel uncomfortable about it. They realize the irony of their position. In asserting the independence of their own news judgment, they are, in effect, asserting their right to be used by the terrorists.

6

MAINTAINING INDEPENDENCE FROM THE GOVERNMENT

The A.S.N.E. declares that the press has a duty to "bring an independent scrutiny to bear on the forces of power in society." The government is the most powerful of all those "forces of power," and the one with the most tools for undermining, and potentially crushing, the independence of the press. For that reason, some journalists have long considered the government the greatest real threat to the independence of the press. They have the example of the government-controlled press in countries like the Soviet Union, several of the right-wing dictatorships of Latin America, and many African countries to warn them of the dangers.

In many countries, in fact, the press is little more than a propaganda agency for the government. Journalists are employed by the government and are expected to follow its orders, especially when reporting on governmental affairs. The press in the United States, on the other hand, has remained remarkably independent. The First Amendment has proved to be a powerful, although not invincible, shield for the press. Even despite it, however, the government has sometimes attempted to move against the press with all the force of law behind it.

CENSORSHIP

In the Sedition Act of 1798, for example, Congress made it a crime to print (or to utter) scandalous or malicious statements against the government, or to "conspire" to bring it "into contempt or disrepute." Since the Federalist Party controlled the government at that time, the effect of the act was to make it a crime to criticize the Federalists in print. The law was aimed squarely at the Democratic-Republican press, and in fact several Democratic-Republican editors were actually put in jail under it. They were, not surprisingly, released by the next Democratic-Republican president, Thomas Jefferson, and the act was allowed to expire.

In the years prior to the outbreak of World War I, hundreds of German-language newspapers were published in the United States, particularly in states like Wisconsin and Pennsylvania, which had large populations of German immigrants who still spoke (and read) their own language. Once war with Germany was declared, these papers came under heavy suspicion from the government. Many closed.

Some 2,000 people, many of them journalists, were prosecuted under a new Sedition Act. Prominent among them were several editors and contributors to the *Masses*, a New York based, English-language magazine that regularly published some of the leading literary talents of the age—among them Sherwood Anderson, Carl Sandburg, and Upton Sinclair—most of whom wrote for the magazine without payment. The *Masses* had no ties with Germany, or even with the German-American community, but it was both Socialist and anti-war in its editorial positions. The defendants each faced a potential sentence of twenty years in jail and a $10,000 fine for what they had written

*Two views of freedom
of the press*

WINNER OF THE
WARREN E. BURGER
AWARD
FOR **EXCELLENCE**
IN **JOURNALISM.**

GORRELL 1978 THE NEWS-PRESS
ROTHCO

I'LL TELLS YA WHAT I THINK OF THE AMERICAN PRESS: IT STINKS!

THEY SHOULD PRINT WHAT THE GOVERNMENT TELLS 'EM, AN' STOP ASKIN' QUESTIONS. IF THEY CANT SAY ANYTHIN' NICE, THEN THEY OUGHT TO KEEP THEIR YAPS SHUT! JUST THINK...

...WHAT A WONDERFUL PLACE THIS WOULD BE IF OUR PRESS WUZ RUN LIKE TH' SOVIETS'.

KIRK ROTHCO
©1983 THE SCRANTON TIMES

opposing the war. They only escaped conviction by one vote, when the jury was hung eleven to one against them.[1]

In 1971, the federal government tried to stop the *New York Times* from publishing excerpts from the so-called Pentagon Papers, a top-secret study of American involvement in Vietnam that had been commissioned by the Pentagon itself. When the *Times* began to publish the Papers, the government persuaded a judge to issue an injunction ordering it to stop. But when the paper appealed, the Supreme Court overturned the injunction as a violation of press freedom. Such pre-censorship was held to be unconstitutional by a majority of the judges, although they didn't agree among themselves about the reasoning behind their rulings.[2] The Court did not rule out prosecution of the newspaper *after* publication, however. (As it turned out, the *Times* was not prosecuted, although the two people who had given the classified material to the paper were. Their cases were eventually dismissed because the government had violated their constitutional rights in various ways while trying to develop the case against them.)

One of the most extreme cases of governmental action against a journalist was that of Samuel Loring Morison, who was convicted in 1985 of violating the Espionage Act of 1917. He had sent the British magazine *Jane's Defense Weekly*, of which he was an editor, American spy-satellite pictures of a Soviet shipyard, along with information about some accidental damage that had been done to a Soviet missile base. The pictures had been classified (as the Pentagon Papers had been) and the information had been obtained from American intelligence reports.[3] He is still in jail.

Such direct governmental attempts to control the press, to intimidate it, or to punish it have been relatively rare in American history. Still, the threat of government action is always there. It may be less immediate than the threat hanging over journalists in many other countries, but as the above cases show (and others could be mentioned), it is real.

Critics of the press may argue that this threat is appropriate. They feel that because of the strong tradition of freedom of the press in this country, the government can be counted on to move against the press only in cases of extreme necessity. The first Sedition Act was passed at a time when American ships were being threatened by France, the second Sedition Act was brought about by the First World War, and the Pentagon Papers case came during the Vietnam War. At such times, these journalists feel, the wishes of the government should be respected. If some elements of the press are so stubborn—or so unpatriotic—that they act against the interests of their own government in time of war or national emergency, they deserve to be prosecuted. These critics argue, in effect, that the journalists have an ethical responsibility as citizens to help keep the government's secrets, and when ethical responsibility as a citizen comes in conflict with ethical responsibility as a journalist, duty as a citizen must take precedence.

Other journalists, however, would argue that there is no conflict between their responsibilities as citizens and as journalists. Both require them to publish whatever information about government activities they can find. It is the people, and not the government, who are the ultimate authorities in a democracy. The role of the press is to inform the people, whether the government thinks they should have the information or not.

For the most part, in any case, both governmental agencies and individual politicians have usually been content to find ways to use the press to their own advantage, rather than to silence it by censorship.

NATIONAL SECURITY

It is common, whenever the government doesn't want something published, to claim that secrecy is needed for reasons of national security; that is, that publication of the information would damage the ability of the country to defend itself from its enemies.

Such claims are often requests for self-censorship on the part of the press. They are usually made by the military or the White House, to a reporter or to his or her employer, in an effort to convince them not to publish information they already possess. It can be a troublesome problem for conscientious members of the press who take seriously their obligations both as citizens and as journalists.

Clearly there is such a thing as national security, and clearly the publication of certain pieces of information could place it in jeopardy.

Most reporters will at least consider requests for self-censorship in the interest of national security, and several cases have come to light of journalists bowing to those requests. The prominent journalist James Reston has acknowledged that he kept quiet about secret U-2 spy plane flights over the Soviet Union in 1959, for example. And both the *New York Times* and the *New Republic* magazine knew about plans for the CIA-supported invasion of Cuba at the Bay of Pigs in 1961, and kept them secret.[4]

Not all reporters would have agreed to keep those particular secrets, but most would probably admit that the claim of national security was at least arguable in those cases. Some agencies and presidential administrations have made much less defensible claims. In Richard Nixon's administration, for example, national security was used as a blanket excuse, not only for secrecy, but for government wiretaps, burglaries, and other illegal acts. Those acts, it turned out, had been committed primarily to help Nixon's own re-election campaign. For the people in the Nixon White House, apparently, national security and Richard Nixon's political future were the same.

Most administrations are not that self-serving in their application of the principle, although all of them tend to apply it more broadly than most journalists would. They feel that it is presumptuous of journalists to reserve the right to make their own decisions in cases of national security. That, they say, should be left up to the president or his agents. The reporter may know a given fact, or set of facts, but only the president knows *all* the facts surrounding the situation. Therefore only he can decide whether the national security would be threatened by their release.

Some journalists would reject almost any claim of national security out of hand, although they would be careful with information that could threaten American lives. It is unlikely, they say, that the national security would be seriously damaged by anything reported in the American press. Rarely, if ever, can the press get hold of information America's enemies can't get as well. They point to the claims of national security made for America's secret bombing of Cambodia during the Vietnam War. Clearly, the Cambodians and their allies knew that they were being bombed. The real purpose of the secrecy was to hide the truth about America's actions from the American public. And, they say, the national security can never be protected by doing that.

Even in the two cases described earlier, in which honorable journalists agreed to keep the government's secrets, it is hard to see how national security was served in the end. The U-2 spy plane flights eventually did become public knowledge, but not through revelations in the press. Instead, the Soviet Union exposed them by shooting down one of the planes over their territory. Not only was it a serious international embarrassment for the United States, but it ruined the chances for a productive summit conference that was to be held in Paris between U.S. President Dwight Eisenhower and Soviet Premier Nikita Khrushchev. Similarly, the Bay of Pigs invasion turned out to be a costly and bloody failure. People close to the then President, John F. Kennedy (and, some say, Kennedy himself) later regretted that the secret had *not* come out before the invasion. It might have caused it to be called off. The president, and the country, might have been spared a military fiasco, and many lives might have been saved.

PRESIDENTS

Presidents have enormous advantages when it comes to using the press. Unlike most politicians, the president does not have to scramble for press attention. Everything about a president is news: where he (and someday she) goes, what he does, and what he says.

Any time a president wants access to the press he can have it, and usually on his own terms. If he wants pictures of himself to appear on television or in the newspapers, he only has to hold what is called a "photo opportunity"—an appearance where it has been announced that he will make himself available for pictures to be taken. Film, television, and still photographers will flock to the event, and his picture will probably appear in the media all across the country as a result.

If he wants to speak to the people, all he usually has to do is to ask for television time and chances are that all the major networks will carry his address live and in prime time. (Such presidential requests have been denied by the television networks, but only rarely.) If he doesn't wish to speak at length, he can give a brief quote to virtually any reporter, or group of reporters, he wishes. If his words are at all significant, or even catchy, they will be widely reported.

If, on the other hand, a president doesn't want to speak at all, there is virtually no way the press can force him to do so. Some presidents have been known to go for months without speaking at any length to the press. Woodrow Wilson and Ronald Reagan are two presidents who have frozen out the press for long periods of time.

Some journalists are troubled by the press's role in this relationship. They worry that, instead of being the watchdogs they were meant to be, reporters who cover the president become publicists for whoever occupies the office. They feel that the press has an obligation to resist being used in this way by the president.

One way to resist is to demand a higher standard of newsworthiness before covering presidential activities. Another is to subject presidential remarks to more critical scrutiny than is usually the case today.

Theodore Roosevelt called the presidency a "bully pulpit." By that he meant that it provided a wonderful position from which to speak to the people and to persuade them to the president's point of view. Whatever the president says is widely quoted by the press and is taken seriously by the public at large. If that was true when Roosevelt was president (1901 to 1909), the pervasiveness of radio and television has made it even truer today. In the past, even presidents had to rely largely on excerpts and quotes in the printed press. Such quotes were often printed (at least in the opposition press) side by side with attacks on the president by rival politicians. Today, presidents can speak to the people directly over the electronic media.

Most presidential comments are published, whether quoted in print or broadcast electronically, without journalistic commentary. This is largely true even when a president says things which are clearly inaccurate, or even deliberately misleading. Some journalists, including James L. Hoyt, Director of the University of Wisconsin's School of Journalism and Mass Communications, believe that the press needs to be more critical. Hoyt believes that when a president (or any other politician, for that matter) makes an error of fact, the press should not report that statement without pointing out that it is in error. He further believes that if the president is contradicting himself—saying one thing to appeal to one audience and the opposite to appeal to another—the press has a duty to point this out as well.[5]

Some journalists are reluctant to do this. They feel that it is presumptuous for a reporter to "take on" the president in this way. Or they fear that such criticism would open them up to charges of political bias and hostility to the president. Others argue that to quote a presidential

*Former president Lyndon B. Johnson
with reporters at his ranch in 1964.*

error uncritically, or to participate in a presidential deception of the public, would be a serious violation of the journalists' ethical responsibility.

Some presidents are masters at courting the press. Andrew Jackson was so close to a number of powerful newspapermen that they were commonly referred to as his "Kitchen Cabinet." A few presidents, like Warren G. Harding and John F. Kennedy, had once been newspapermen themselves, and so were exceptionally good at dealing with journalists.

Lyndon Johnson was probably the most hard working and original president of recent times when it came to courting the press. Where another president might invite a reporter to dinner at the White House, Johnson would take carloads of reporters around his large Texas ranch, driving them himself in his own car, and personally serving them beer and pointing out the sights along the way.

On the other hand, presidents have sometimes been known to take reporters to task for stories they didn't like. Once again, Johnson's example was among the most extreme. He was known to make angry phone calls to editors, often in the middle of the night, waking them up to complain angrily about an unfavorable story and pressuring them to punish the offending journalists.

Just how effective these presidential efforts to influence the press actually are is open to debate. Certainly it must be hard to ignore either praise or blame from a president of the United States.

Ethically, of course, journalists are expected to resist both flattery and intimidation, even from presidents. Few of them would admit to being seriously influenced by either. And yet, presidents continue to court the press. They, at least, seem to feel that they are getting something in return for their efforts.

7

PLAYING FAIR

The principle of fairness is an extremely wide-ranging one. For a journalist, its implications extend in many directions—to colleagues, subjects, sources, and the public at large—and give rise to a wide range of ethical issues. Although a whole book could probably be written analyzing the ethical implications of any one of those issues, we will only be able to discuss a few of them here, and at relatively short length. It would be well to keep in mind, however, a statement from the Standards and Ethics code of the *Washington Post*: "While arguments about objectivity are endless, the concept of fairness is something that editors and reporters can easily understand and pursue."[1]

PLAGIARISM

In a sense, a journalist who commits *any* violation of professional ethics is not playing fair with his or her fellow journalists. Every ethical failure reflects badly not only on the journalist involved, and on his or her own news organization, but on the profession of journalism in general. Some unethical practices, however, directly violate the rights of other journalists. Of these, the most obvious is plagiarism.

Plagiarism is the unfair, and unauthorized, use of other people's work, passed off as your own. A reporter, finding a good story in a newspaper or magazine, simply copies all or part of it, and submits it for publication as his or her own. Sometimes the reporter will alter the material slightly in order to disguise its source. At other times, if the source is distant or obscure enough, the material will be taken whole, without any changes whatsoever.

Plagiarism is probably the most universally condemned of all the ethical violations among journalists themselves. Fully 99 percent of editors responding to the A.S.N.E. survey disapproved of the practice. This is hardly surprising. Plagiarism is unfair both to the original source of the material and to the news organization to which it is submitted. The original author has certain rights to his or her own material, and, in general, it should not be used by anyone without attribution, or, in some cases, actual permission. If the publication or broadcast in which the material was presented was copyrighted, those rights are protected by law. At the same time, the plagiarizer's employer has the right to expect honest and independent work from his or her employee.

On the other hand, the line between plagiarism and fair journalistic use of published material can be difficult to draw. Once a story has been published or broadcast, the facts in that story become a part of the public domain. That is, they are public knowledge, and can be used by anyone without authorization from the original source. Only the expression of those facts, the way the facts were presented, or the story written, is protected by copyright.

Sometimes journalists will rework stories from other sources. In certain circumstances this can be done ethically, even without attribution or payment; but a journalist reworking a story is expected to change it significantly, not only expressing the facts differently, but adding to the story in some useful and important way. Ninety-six percent of the surveyed editors objected to their reporters' rewriting a story without verifying the facts in the story independently. When possible, new facts should be developed as well. A local angle might be included. Fresh quotes can be sought from participants or authorities to give the story a new perspective, and so on. Once a story has been reworked sufficiently, and made the reporter's own, with no extensive direct quotes from the original used without acknowledgment and permission, there is no longer any question of plagiarism involved.

Unfortunately, no reliable standard is available to determine exactly when that point has been reached. Initially, it is up to each reporter and editor to determine for themselves what is and what is not fair use. And that is a question on which the judgments of individuals can, and often do, differ. Ultimately, when a dispute arises the courts may have to decide whether the standard of fair use has been violated.

LIBEL

The First Amendment gives the press a great deal of latitude, but it does not protect journalists in falsely and unfairly attacking the reputations of individuals. That is called libel, and it has always been considered a kind of exception to the First Amendment. Victims of libel can go to court and sue the journalist or news organization who libeled them.

In order to do so, however, the plaintiff has to prove several things: first, that the libel referred to him or her, and that this was apparent in the story; second, that the libel was false; third, that it was defamatory (that is, that it held the victim up to public hatred, ridicule, or contempt); and fourth, that it resulted in real damage to the victim, either a loss of the victim's good reputation, or a financial loss, or both.

The Supreme Court has made the standard for proving

"Oh, excuse me, for a moment
I thought you were Carol Burnett!"

libel even higher when the person claiming to be libeled is a public official. Officials, the Court ruled in *Times* v. *Sullivan* in 1964, have to prove that the libel was published either "with actual malice—that is, the knowledge that it was false—or with reckless disregard of whether it was false or not."[2] In practice, that ruling has been extended to include many celebrities who, although not public officials, are still regarded as public figures.

Even with that difficult standard to protect it, a number of highly publicized libel cases have been lost by the press in recent years. Three of the most famous of them involved the actress and comedienne Carol Burnett, one-time commander of United States troops in Vietnam General William Westmoreland, and Israeli General Ariel Sharon.[3]

Few, if any, reputable journalists would argue that they have an ethical right to falsely defame anyone. They recognize the need to apply the ordinary demands of truth and accuracy with spécial care when the reputatíons of private citizens are at stake. But exactly how careful one has to be is always a matter of judgment.

From the Burnett, Westmoreland, and Sharon cases—and from the fact that the proportion of libel cases won by the plaintiffs seems to be rising—it can be argued that there is a gap between the public's standards for libel and that of the press, and that the gap is growing. It is, after all, members of the public who sit on the juries.

For journalists, there are two very different ethical dimensions to the question of libel. One, of course, is the need to avoid committing it. The other is the need to avoid being intimidated by the threat that the libel laws will be used against them. Many journalists are convinced that the libel laws are being used for that purpose in many cases today: not to protect innocent reputations, but to intimidate—and ultimately to silence—the press.

Libel suits are apt to be long, difficult, expensive, and time consuming. Recognizing this, individuals and groups who want to "scare off" the press (or to punish the press for a story already printed) can bring libel suits against it. Even if those suits are frivolous, they can harass a reporter or news organization, and in some cases even bankrupt them. The threat of repeated court actions, however unjustified those actions might be, can be chillingly effective.

It is not just journalists who see this danger. Judge Robert Bork of the United States Court of Appeals put it this way: "In the past few years a remarkable upsurge in libel actions, accompanied by a startling inflation in damage awards, has threatened to impose a self-censorship on the press which can as effectively inhibit debate and criticism as would overt government regulation that the First Amendment certainly would not permit."[4]

The threat is particularly powerful when it is made against small news organizations. Large institutions, like the *New York Times* (the defendant in the Sharon case) and CBS Television News (the defendant in the Westmoreland case), can afford to fight a long and difficult court battle. The small-town newspaper or television station cannot. As a result, many journalists, particularly among small-town publishers and editors, see the current libel laws as presenting a real threat to journalistic freedom, and a real challenge to their own independence and courage.

MISREPRESENTATIONS

In their efforts to gather news, journalists sometimes deceive people, pretending to be something other than they are in order to elicit information. Such deceptions raise serious ethical concerns.

There are various degrees of deception. At one end of the ethical scale, a reporter may take advantage of someone else's mistake. Arriving at the scene of a crime, for example, he or she might be taken for a plainclothes police officer, and use that misunderstanding to question witnesses.

The degree of deception goes up if the reporter initiates the deception by deliberately acting like a police offi-

cer. Still a further ethical line is crossed if the reporter actually identifies him- or herself as a police officer.

Some reporters have actually gone undercover, taking on entirely false identities in order to get information that would never be available to an admitted reporter. Reporters have lived as homeless people, in order to report on the life of the indigent, and as drug addicts, to find out what life is like in the drug scene of a major city. In one famous example of undercover reporting, a young reporter named Gloria Steinem (later a founding editor of *Ms* magazine) hid her journalistic intentions and took a job as a Playboy bunny in order to write about the bunnies' working conditions in *Show* magazine.[5] In an earlier case, a white writer named John Howard Griffin disguised himself as black in order to describe to his fellow whites what life was like for a black man in a segregated America in a book called *Black Like Me*.[6]

Some journalists frown on any kind of deception. They believe that reporters should always declare themselves as members of the press. Not to do so, they feel, is to deal with people under false pretenses. It is a kind of fraud, even a kind of theft: eliciting information, for publication, from sources who would not willingly give it for that purpose.

Other journalists believe that the comparison between information and personal property won't hold. There is no property right to hoard information. Besides, they say, the journalist's obligation to gather the news, along with the value to society of reporting it, more than justify a certain amount of deception.

Reporters justify deceptions in two main ways. The first is the importance of the story. The second is the argument that some stories cannot be obtained in any other way. Some journalists believe that the second is the most important justification for undercover reporting. Deception, they believe, can only be justified when it is the *only* way that the reporter can get a particular story.

One of the most elaborate, and morally most questionable, forms of deception is the journalistic sting operation. "Sting" is a term used by con artists to mean setting someone up in order to cheat them. To the journalist, it means setting someone up in order to catch them doing something wrong.

Stings can be either simple or elaborate. An example of the simple kind took place in Minneapolis, Minnesota, where a local television station placed unguarded bicycles in a number of spots around the city to tempt bicycle thieves. Hidden cameramen proceeded to take television pictures of children stealing the bikes.[7]

A more elaborate sting took place in Chicago, where the *Sun-Times* set up an entire neighborhood bar and staffed it with reporters. It was an area of known graft and corruption and, as the reporters planned, many local and state officials came around asking for bribes. The bribes were paid, while *Sun-Times* photographers took pictures of the transactions. When the operation was over, the paper had a sensational twenty-five part series exposing widespread corruption and resulting in the disclosure of a number of corrupt officials.[8]

Like most cases of journalistic deception, these stings were controversial. Several of the general arguments given above might be made for and against both of them. But they raise a new ethical issue as well. That is because they resulted in—and were intended to result in—criminal acts. They could be seen, in fact, as deliberate plots to incite people to commit crimes.

In their defense, neither the television reporters in Minneapolis nor the newspaper reporters in Chicago actually asked anyone to commit a crime. They merely provided the opportunity. But the fact remains that the specific criminal acts exposed would not have been committed at all if the reporters had not deliberately offered the criminals an occasion to commit them.

FAKING STORIES

In April of 1981, a twenty-six-year-old reporter named Janet Cooke was awarded the prestigious Pulitzer Prize in Journalism for a feature story entitled "Jimmy's World," which had appeared in the *Washington Post*. Later that same week, the *Post* gave the prize back. It had discovered that the story, an account of an eight-year-old heroin addict named Jimmy, was a fake. Janet Cooke had made up the story—and Jimmy.[9]

The sensational news shocked those members of the public who had a basic faith in the integrity of major press institutions like the *Post*, and it confirmed the worst suspicions of those who did not. It also demonstrated what virtually all journalists know, but few like to talk about—that reporters sometimes invent things.

Usually it is not the central fact in a story, as it was in

(Some people believe that Bob Woodward,
one of the two reporters who broke
the Watergate scandal, made up some
of the information in his recent book
on former CIA director William Casey.)

"Jimmy's World." More often, it is a piece of evidence that substantiates such a central fact, or a nonexistent source, a manufactured quote, or a minor piece of information that lends color to a story.

Since these inventions are, by definition, deceptions, there is no way to tell how widespread this practice actually is. Certain major instances have come to light, but most remain undiscovered.

It can be argued—and probably the vast majority of reputable journalists would agree—that any faking of information is too much. It is also possible to argue, however, that a certain amount of invention, under certain circumstances, ought to be permissible.

Out-and-out hoaxes were a staple of nineteenth-century journalism. Newspapers would print them in a deliberate effort to attract readers. The most famous was the "Moonbat" hoax published by the New York Sun in 1835. Purporting to be publishing actual scientific observations of a Scottish scientist, the Sun announced that telescopic investigation had discovered bat-like creatures living on the moon. The story was presented with great seriousness, and tens of thousands of people, including many scientists, believed it. When the hoax was eventually discovered, the paper defended what it had done with the argument that the story had entertained its readers, and taken the public's mind off more serious affairs.

Few news organizations would publish a similar hoax today, except perhaps on April Fools' Day.

But some journalists argue that certain kinds of invention are not only acceptable but desirable, when they contribute to the essential truth of a story. These might include: re-creating conversations between subjects of a news story that approximate conversations that must have occurred; putting in the form of a quote the reporter's idea of what the subject of a story might have said in a given situation; and describing the place where something occurred, or the people involved, or the events themselves, in more detail than the reporter actually had available.[10]

These are essentially fiction-writing techniques. They have been adopted by practitioners of what used to be called the "new journalism" or the "new nonfiction," including such famous authors as Truman Capote, Tom Wolfe, and Norman Mailer. Ironically, they are all techniques common in the *old* journalism of the nineteenth century. Some reporters (presumably including those mentioned above) would defend their use in modern journalism on the grounds that they add to the public's understanding of a story. They help the public imagine the reality of the events more clearly, or at least more intensely, than they would be able to from a dry, though slavishly accurate account.

Even some journalists who dislike these techniques might accept them, but only in clearly labeled stories, in which it is explained that they are being used. Others would object to them even then. At best, such stories are a confusion of reality and invention, and that, these journalists would say, is fiction, not journalism.

A CHANCE TO RESPOND

The final requirement of journalistic fairness is the right to reply. Members of the public who wish to respond to the press—whether merely because they feel the need to react, or because they feel personally injured by something that has appeared in the press—should have the opportunity to do so.

Many news organizations have a policy of not carrying charges against individuals without giving them an opportunity to respond. Even before a story is published, they call up the subject of the story and ask for any denial or explanation he or she would like to make.

Most newspapers have a regular feature made up of letters from members of the public. Those most concerned with the public's right to respond try to keep this letters column as open as possible. Some small papers, with relatively few readers, will print any and all letters that come in to them. They make no restrictions on the letters printed, except to limit length and edit out libel or vulgar language. Even larger papers may choose at least a portion of the letters they print at random.

Some television networks and stations have made efforts to adopt a form of this practice. Some have had their own personnel read from viewer letters. Others have allowed members of the public to appear on air and reply to what they have seen. For the most part, however, these efforts have been less than successful. Because of the premium placed on time in the broadcast media, only a few responses were ever read, and even those were often edited by the station or network. They could hardly be considered a fair representation of viewer response. When amateurs were invited to appear in person, they rarely made effective advocates for their points of view. Besides, it was up to the station or network to decide which amateurs would be allowed to speak. In other words, they were allowed to choose their own critics. Whether for these or other reasons, many of these efforts to let viewers respond on air have been discontinued.

Nonetheless it is generally accepted by modern journalists that a member of the public who points out an error in a news story deserves to see that error corrected. The ethical codes of Sigma Delta Chi, the Society of Professional Journalists, insist not only that "it is the duty of the news media to make prompt and complete correction of their errors" but that "journalists should be accountable to the public for their reports and the public should be encouraged to voice its grievances against the media."[11]

For a long time, newspapers were extremely reluctant to admit errors—whether those errors were errors of fact or errors of ethics. They feared that to do so would damage their credibility. In recent years, however, a number of major papers have embraced the practice of confessing errors, not only of fact but of judgment. Some have employed ombudsmen, watchdogs to deal with readers' complaints, and to take the paper to task, in its own pages, whenever it has violated the ethical standards of good journalism. Most of these papers seem to feel that their credibility has, if anything, been helped rather than hurt by their new openness.

Still, only a relatively small number of newspapers employ ombudsmen, and the rest of the news media has failed to follow their lead.[12]

8

SLANTING
THE NEWS

One of the most common charges made against the press is that it slants the news: that press coverage is colored in ways that prejudice the way the reader (or listener, or viewer) responds.

In a sense, it is impossible for press coverage *not* to be slanted, at least to some degree. At every step in the process of collecting and reporting news, choices have to be made: what stories to cover, what pictures to use, what nouns and adjectives to employ. Each of those choices has some effect on how the public will perceive the news story, and the people and events described in it.

BIAS

Many people believe that the news coverage they receive is politically biased, that the reality of events is seriously distorted by the news media to favor one political point of view or to discredit another.

This raises two important questions. First, is the charge true? And, second, if it is true, is biased news coverage unethical?

"On the other hand, because of the
biased and distorted reportage of Third
World matters by the influential
Western news media, maybe we only
THINK life is lousy here."

In regard to the first, there is little doubt that some news coverage is biased. Certainly individual journalists are biased. Everyone who has an opinion is biased, and journalists have as many opinions as anyone else. But most journalists would argue that they try very hard to keep their personal biases out of their news coverage, and that they usually succeed.

Interestingly, people who charge the press with bias tend to believe that it is biased against their own political point of view, whatever that point of view may be.[1] Conservatives believe that the press has a liberal bias, liberals that it has a conservative bias. And the more extreme a person's political beliefs are, it seems, the stronger the person's conviction that the press is unfair to those beliefs.

The tendency to see the press as biased against one's own point of view is easily understandable. When what people see in the press supports their beliefs they don't perceive what they see as biased. When it challenges—or flatly contradicts—their beliefs, they tend to perceive it as biased.

Two similarly named organizations reflect this natural tendency. The first, called Accuracy in Media (AIM), was founded by Reed Irvine in 1969 specifically to "expose" what it considers the news media's profoundly liberal bias. But AIM itself is far from politically neutral. Irvine has honestly described his organization as "ideological,"[2] and its ideology is clearly conservative and opposed to the liberalism it claims to find in the national media. The second group, Fairness and Accuracy in Reporting (FAIR), was founded by people of liberal views, and works to show what it considers the conservative bias reflected in the national news media.

Journalists are fond of saying, "We are attacked from both sides of the political spectrum, so we must be doing something right." The logic is less than convincing. The fact that people on two different sides of an issue find bias in the press is hardly good evidence that it isn't there. What it does suggest is that if there is an overall bias in the news, it may be toward the political middle of the road, toward positions that favor compromise and moderation. The strongest bias in the American press may be a negative one—a bias against any strongly ideological political position.

What's Wrong with Bias?

To what extent should the political bias that exists in the news be considered unethical? In the early days of American journalism, it was not considered unethical at all. Most early newspapers, in fact, were founded specifically to promote a particular point of view, and they made little distinction between reporting events and arguing political positions.

Today, however, a premium is put on impartiality. Editorial commentary is expected to be kept wholly separate from news reporting, and clearly labeled as such.

This separation came about largely for economic reasons. It began when newspapers began to compete for larger audiences. Instead of continuing to direct themselves only to members of a particular political group, as they had in the past, they tried to appeal to everyone. As a result, they began to shy away from controversial reporting and heavy political commentary. They tried to produce news accounts which would not offend anyone, no matter what their political views. This move toward impartiality was encouraged even further by the development of news services, which sold stories and features to papers of all political persuasions. More and more, a premium was placed on those stories which reported facts accurately, without any particular viewpoint on those facts showing through. The newspapers that bought the stories could add their own viewpoints to them—or not—as they wished.

Eventually, the ethics of news reporting adapted to reflect the changes that had already taken place for economic reasons. The unbiased, strictly factual report became the ideal.

Some people feel that this is a bad thing. They believe

the press's role is not just to inform society, but to move it. They favor what is sometimes called advocacy journalism—reporting that takes a side and attempts to stir the public to action. The press has often been an engine of reform in American society, they say, and it should not give up that role in the name of objectivity. Certainly what is reported should be factual and accurate, but it should also be heartfelt and passionate.

Lincoln Steffens, the turn-of-the-century muckraker, expressed his view of the journalistic urge this way: "I am not a scientist. I am a journalist . . . [My purpose was] to see if the shameful facts, spread out in all their shame, would not burn through our civic shamelessness and set fire to American pride. That was the journalism of it. I wanted to move and to convince."

Most journalists today would disagree. Advocacy, they say, is fine for the editorial pages, and for political columns, when clearly labeled as the opinions of specific writers. It is out of place on the news pages, or in the reports of television and radio reporters. The line between news and opinion should be kept clear. To blur it would be a great mistake. If news reporting is seen as biased, the public will lose trust in it, and the press will have lost its greatest asset.

SOME WAYS NEWS
STORIES ARE SLANTED

Any journalist who wants to slant a news story has a wide range of techniques at his or her command.

Perhaps the most basic, and most powerful, is the choice of which stories to cover. Some stories have to be covered, of course: wars, national elections, major disasters, and the like. But most editors and news directors have a certain amount of space and time at their discretion. They can choose among a variety of possible stories to fill them. Their choices can have a significant effect on the public's perception of the news.

Imagine, for example, two editors of rival newspapers

in the same city. The first supports the current city administration. The second opposes it. The first paper runs three stories on three successive days: the first tells of an important new business venture in the city, one that will employ hundreds of people; the second tells of a successful crackdown on drug dealing in the central city; the third is a long interview with the mayor, in which she describes the many achievements of the current administration.

The second paper also runs three stories: one about a poor family thrown out of their home because the city housing project they were living in has been condemned; one discussing the dramatic rise in violent crime in the central city; and the third, an interview with the head of a citizen's group complaining about the deteriorating quality of the city's garbage collection.

Each of the stories chosen by the editors could be justified as being newsworthy and accurate. But the readers of each paper would be given a very different view of the city and its administration. Readers of the first would see a dynamic city with excellent leadership. Readers of the second would see a city in crisis, with an incompetent and bumbling city government.

The perspective chosen for a story can also affect the readers' perceptions. An account of a criminal trial told from the defendant's point of view would have a very different impact than one told from the viewpoint of the prosecutor.

The omission, or inclusion, of key information can drastically shift the slant of a story. The thrust of a story about a police officer who shot and killed a man stopped for a minor traffic violation would be very different, depending on whether it included the fact that the man had had a gun and had fired first.

All kinds of choices in the wording of a story color its effects. A newspaper reader would get a very different feeling about a man reported as "snarling" or "growling" something, than one reported simply as "saying" it, even if the words quoted were exactly the same.

Pictures can have a telling effect on the way newspaper readers and television viewers perceive people. An unflattering picture can make a person look seedy, or even sinister. A flattering picture, on the other hand, can make a person look cleancut and impressive.

TELEVISION TECHNIQUES

Television has a large variety of potentially unfair practices of its own. In print media interviews, the journalist asking the questions is neither seen nor heard. On television, he or she is an important element of the story. When a popular television journalist addresses the subject of an interview in a hostile manner, that hostility is transmitted to the viewer. A raised eyebrow in response to an answer can effectively suggest disbelief. Conversely, a warm smile and friendly manner can suggest to the viewer that the subject of *this* interview can be trusted and believed.

A question itself can be used to discredit a subject. When a television journalist looks into the camera and asks some version of the old lawyer's question—"Is it true that you've stopped beating your wife?"—it hardly matters what the subject answers.

Television news often prides itself on its balance, on presenting spokespeople for different sides of a public issue, and giving each a chance to have their say. But even this supposed proof of objectivity can be used as a weapon with which to prejudice the public's perception of the issue. Some spokespeople are attractive, some are not. Some are well-groomed, some are scruffy. Some are moderate in the way they express their views, others are extreme. Some speak well and grammatically, others are less educated and stumble over their words. Some speak calmly and quietly, others shout. It is easy for viewers to confuse their reaction to what someone is saying on television with their reaction to the person saying it. By showing only attractive, well-groomed and well-spoken people on one side of an issue, and only unattractive and inarticu-

late people on the other, the impression can be given that one side of the issue is reasonable and moderate, while the other side is extreme and fanatic.

Another technique peculiar to television is the ambush interview. A television reporter and crew bear down on a potential subject unannounced, demanding an interview on the spot. This is often a deliberate effort to make the subject look bad, done in the expectation that the subject will angrily refuse to be interviewed, which is something that any citizen has a perfect right to do. But when the angry refusal is broadcast, it gives the strong impression—often false—that the subject has something to hide.

MAKING CHOICES

Some of the techniques discussed above are unavoidable. Words and pictures must be chosen, and any choice will be influenced by the opinions and prejudices of the person making it. Some, like the ambush interview, can be rejected by journalists who believe that they are unethical. (Not all journalists disapprove of all such techniques.) But in a society dedicated to the freedom of the press, most journalists—even those who strongly disapprove of these techniques—would argue that it would be wrong for the government to legislate against them.

Critics, however, respond that if journalists will not apply ethical standards to themselves, it may be necessary for society to apply such standards by law. The First Amendment, they say, does not give a blanket license to unfairness, bias, and deliberate slanting of the news.

An all-American photograph of Oliver North and his family. The clean-cut image does not negate the fact that he illegally shredded official government documents.

9

SELLING THE NEWS
OR SELLING OUT?

As we have seen, the integrity of the press is threatened from many directions, including the interference of government and the unethical practices of some journalists themselves. But some critics of the press see even these threats as relatively minor compared to the biggest threat of all: the temptations to corruption that come from commercialism—the need to make money from the news.

The news is a business. Most newspapers are privately owned companies, expected to provide income for their owners. Local television news shows are often the biggest moneymakers their stations have. The major television news departments are merely divisions of large networks, and those networks, in turn, are often merely divisions of much larger conglomerates whose primary function is to make as much money as possible for their stockholders.

Because of this need, few news organizations have the luxury of simply gathering the news as well as they can and then presenting it for anyone who might be interested. They have to produce income—more income than they expend.

Most news organizations make money in one or both of

two main ways. The first is from the people who pay to receive the news: who buy newspapers and magazines, or who subscribe to a cable television news service, for examples. The second is from advertisers, who pay to have their ads or commercials appear in conjunction with the news.

Ultimately, both ways depend on attracting an audience for the news, whether to pay for it directly or to draw the advertisers who will pay to reach them. This means that the media have to present the news in a way that will draw large enough audiences to produce a profit. The news beomes a product, and journalists become salespeople. Their job—or at least one of their jobs— is to sell the news.

JOURNALISTIC
SEX APPEAL

It was circulation wars that resulted in the excesses of the penny press back in the nineteenth century, and the need to attract as many readers, viewers, or listeners as possible can still exert a corrupting effect on the practice of journalism today. One of the ways this corrupting effect shows itself is in the selection of stories to be covered by the press.

An uncounted number of newsworthy events take place all over the world every day. And every day, newspeople have to decide which of those events to report. Space in newspapers and magazines is limited. Time on national radio and television is even more limited. Choices have to be made.

One factor influencing those choices is, which of those events is the most entertaining? Which has the most commercial "sex appeal"? Which will grab the attention of the greatest number of people and get them to buy the publication or stay tuned to the news show?

Entertaining, in this sense, does not necessarily mean light-hearted, or frivolous. Not all popular movies are comedies, after all. There are thrillers, tear-jerkers, and horror movies as well. In much the same way, news stories that inspire excitement, invite sympathy, or incite fear can be even more entertaining than those that arouse laughter.

At times, the most entertaining story of the day may also be the most significant. There are some things that virtually everyone is eager to know about—the results of a presidential election, for example, the outbreak of a war, the signing of a peace treaty, a sudden boom (or bust) in the stock market. But, more often, the story that has the most sex appeal and the one that has the most significance are not the same. And too often, critics charge, it is the story with the most sex appeal that will win out in the battle for prominence in the news media.

Economic competition has been helping to shape the nature of journalism for a long time. It was the competition for readers among the "penny papers" of the early nineteenth century that produced many of the elements that are staples of the modern news business. Human interest stories, tourism and travel coverage, entertainment news—all were first introduced back then. Even crime news was first emphasized in American newspapers not because the editors thought that crime was something people needed to know about, but because it proved to be popular. Crime news was a circulation builder.[1]

These are still the kinds of stories favored by much of the American press today. They are the ones most likely to get the banner headlines on the front pages of the newspapers, to be the leads on the network television news shows, and to be featured on the covers of the weekly news magazines. Other stories that are merely socially, economically, or politically significant, but lacking in popular appeal, are likely to be dealt with more briefly, if at all.

It could be argued that these decisions have little to do with ethics. The decision whether or not to print such stories is a matter of news judgment. And the public's tastes and interests are a valid aspect of news judgment. But

**COPS TO QUIZ
BRIDE'S EX-BEAU**

OUTRAGE!
**Mangled photog's kin pray
cops will nail her attacker**

**HUBBY WIPES OUT
A FAMILY**

**SHOT SLAYS BRONX BOY
Hit While Opening His Gifts**

*These crime headlines are standard fare in
newspapers that use such headlines—with
two-inch-high letters—to sell papers.*

good, ethical journalism requires (among other things) that the journalist exercise responsible news judgment. And what if what the public wants is irresponsible news judgment—news judgment that puts entertainment value ahead of social and political significance, and perhaps ahead of accuracy as well? (Nineteenth-century readers loved the "moonbat" story, remember, even though it wasn't true.) In that case, the public taste can be considered a kind of conflict of interest in itself: a conflict between the journalist's obligation to practice ethical journalism, and the economic need to attract as much of the public as possible.

In this case, the argument that nothing is wrong with giving the public what it wants is a little like the argument made by a reporter charged with any other conflict of interest. ("I wouldn't have used that story about the company's financial troubles, anyway, even if I didn't own stock in the company myself.") The problem, of course, is that there is no way to be sure. The trouble with any conflict of interest is precisely that it confuses the motives, and ultimately the news judgment, of the journalist involved.

SENSATIONALIZING THE NEWS

The need to attract the attention of the public results in a tendency to sensationalize the news: to concentrate on its more thrilling, shocking, or morbid aspects, and to present them in the most dramatic and emotional ways possible.

Sensational news coverage tries to make news events seem either much better or much worse than they really are. When there is an epidemic of a disease, for example, the worst possible estimates of its spread are emphasized. When there is some natural disaster, and there are differing estimates of the number of lives lost, it is the highest estimate which appears in the headline. "SHIP SINKS—HUNDREDS FEARED DEAD!" is more likely to be the headline in a sensational newspaper than "SHIP

SINKS—HUNDREDS RESCUED!" It is likely to sell more papers. At least, many editors and publishers seem to think so. (If anyone doubts this, they can compare the headlines in a big city tabloid, of the kind which is clearly more interested in attracting readers than in practicing serious journalism, to those in a paper like the New York Times.)

The tendency to sensationalism is, if anything, even greater in television than in the print media, because of its immediacy. As the educator and former U.S. Senator, S. I. Hayakawa once said, "Television magnifies everything that goes on television."[2] But television is not the only offender.

On May 3, 1987, the *Miami Herald* charged that ex-Senator Gary Hart had spent the night with a Miami model. Hart, who was already deep into his campaign for the Democratic nomination for president in 1988, was married. The story caused an immediate sensation.[3].

In the wake of the *Herald*'s story, the national media swarmed around Hart, his wife and family, the model, and anyone else who had anything to do with the alleged incident. Facts, rumors, and speculation about the candidate's personal life were on every front page and on nearly every radio and television news report in the country for over a week. Finally, Hart, who had been the leading contender for the nomination, announced that he was quitting the campaign. The press, he said, was interested in nothing but his sex life. It was all they asked him about. They were not interested in—and would not cover—anything else about his campaign, and therefore, he said, it was pointless for him to continue.[4]. He rejoined the race several months later.

The journalists who had covered the story might have argued that it was Hart, and not they, who had created the story; and that it was the public, not they, who was clamoring for more information about the affair. It was a legitimate story, of national interest, and they were ethically bound to cover it.

Critics, however, argued that it was not a legitimate story at all. It was little more than dirty gossip. Among those critics were the majority of people who responded to a Gallup poll taken shortly after the story broke. Fifty-two percent of them felt that the private lives of candidates should be "off limits" to the press, while 64 percent felt that the press had been unfair in its coverage of the Hart story.[5] Nonetheless, papers and news magazines featuring the story seemed to sell very well.

INVASIONS
OF PRIVACY

Gary Hart is not the only person to charge the press with invasion of privacy. Critics charge that the press regularly invades the privacy of those it writes about, and not just in what it reports. Many of the charges involve the practices reporters use in covering the news. Individual people who find themselves at the center of a hot news story can find themselves literally besieged by reporters. Their personal lives (and those of their families) can be totally disrupted.

Richard Allen, the one-time National Security Adviser for President Reagan, found himself in that situation in 1982. He later described what it was like for *Time* magazine: "We were held captive in our house by the media from roughly mid-November to early January. This was all day, every day. Christmas, New Year's, wedding anniversary, birthdays. They would begin to come at about 5:30 in the morning." When he left the house to go to work, the reporters swooped down to press him with questions. They even pestered his daughter. "A CBS reporter tried to question my six-year-old daughter Kimberly, on her way to kindergarten. 'Is your daddy home?' My kids were afraid to go out."[6]

Some of the victims of this kind of treatment find it inexcusable. Many journalists feel uncomfortable about it themselves. And yet, some would argue, it can be justified

when it is the only way reporters have of getting a story. If the people subjected to this kind of siege would only agree to meet with reporters and talk with them, the journalists say, the siege would end. Perhaps, critics answer, but citizens in a free country have the right *not* to talk to the press if they don't want to. Exercising that right should not subject them and their families to merciless harassment.

The press can be equally merciless in its examination of the private lives of celebrities of all kinds, from rock stars to presidents. Their sex lives, marriages, family troubles, and drug and alcohol problems are the staples of some elements of the press. Even the most respectable press institutions have been known to report events like the arrest of a politician's son on a drug charge, or the entry of a well-known actor into an alcohol treatment center, as national news stories. This attention can sometimes border on the cruel, and even the grotesque. In recent years, for instance, press speculation about which male entertainers might have AIDS has come close to the ghoulish.

Journalists use various arguments to justify their intrusiveness. When the subject of that intrusiveness is a politician, they argue that a person's private life can reflect on, and even influence, his or her public policies. If a legislator's spouse has a drug problem, mightn't that affect the legislator's attitudes toward drug legislation? Besides, they say, politicians' private lives may indicate something about their characters. If a married politician is having an affair, don't the voters have a right to know about his or her unfaithfulness? If the politician's own spouse can't trust him or her to keep promises, how can the public?

Besides, some journalists argue, celebrities, whether in politics or show business, have *asked* to be in the public eye. They desperately want people to know them, and to be interested in them. Part of that interest is bound to extend to their private lives. Anyone who sets out to become famous must know that they are going to pay a price for fame, a price that includes journalists prying into their personal affairs.

But that argument doesn't hold for those people who have no wish to be celebrities, who are only thrust into the public eye as a result of circumstances beyond their control. And, critics charge, the press can be every bit as intrusive—and sometimes as cruel—to such people as they sometimes are to movie stars and presidents.

The families of people who are kidnapped, taken hostage, murdered, or caught up in some other kind of tragedy, are often questioned (some would say hounded) by reporters. Microphones are shoved in front of their faces, and they are asked to describe their anger, their fear, or their grief. There have even been cases of television cameramen accompanying officials to the homes of soldiers who have been killed, in order to film family members at the very moment when they are first informed of the tragedy.

People have been photographed in the most extreme situations, writhing in pain after an accident, in the midst of suicide attempts, and even in their death agonies. Pictures of dead bodies, often the victims of violent crimes, have become common in newspapers, newsmagazines, and on television news.

Family members are not spared from the photographic intrusions into their tragedies. When Christa McAuliffe and her fellow astronauts were killed in the explosion of the *Challenger* space shuttle, several members of her family were on the scene to watch the launch. Television and still cameras trained on them caught their shock, terror—and finally their grief—as the rocket lifting *Challenger* blew up before their eyes. A dramatic photograph of their reaction was run in several newspapers the next day. Many people were appalled. One man expressed his objection this way in a telephone call to the *Sacramento Bee*: "There are some moments, even when those moments are in full view, that should remain private, when the press shouldn't intrude."[7]

Some journalists would agree. Others would not. The press's job, they argue, is to present reality, however ugly or painful that reality may be. Dramatic photographs like those of the McAuliffes are justified because they express that reality in a way that words alone could never do.

Certainly the need to express the reality of actual events is a legitimate journalistic motive. But some critics of the press suspect that it is not the real motive behind the press's use of photographs and TV footage of violence, pain, death, and grief. They suspect that the real motive is to appeal to the morbid curiosity of the public—to lure the public with luridness and melodrama, to give them the real-life equivalent of what they go to crime thrillers and slasher movies to see—and by doing so to sell more newspapers and to capture more viewers for the nightly news.

FEARMONGERING

The conservative commentator Irving Kristol once wrote that "The media—and television especially—is most influential during moments of panic and crisis, when people turn to it for instant information. It is therefore as natural for the media to lean toward panic-mongering and crisis-mongering as it is for a plant to lean toward the sunlight."[8]

Some social scientists believe that this "natural" tendency promotes fear and anxiety among the public at large. There is some evidence, for example, that people who watch a lot of television are demonstrably more frightened of street crime than those who do not.

An even more dramatic example of this effect can be seen in the press's handling of international terrorism in the mid-1980s. In 1985 and early '86 there were a number of terrorist attacks in Europe and the Middle East. The majority of the attacks were carried out by Palestinian terrorists angry at the state of Israel and its supporters, including the United States. Several Americans were killed and injured. Not surprisingly, terrorism became a hot subject in the American press.

There was a deluge of news stories about terrorism in virtually all the media. One result was a widespread fear, bordering on panic, among Americans thinking of traveling abroad. Despite the efforts of travel agencies and foreign governments to reassure travelers, large numbers of Americans canceled previous plans to go to Europe and the Middle East. They were simply too afraid to go. This was particularly true in the early summer, after a long winter of media concentration on terrorism. The intensity of the coverage lessened dramatically later in the summer, and foreign tourism picked up again.

Critics charged that by focusing so relentlessly on the

dangers of terrorism, the press made them seem much worse than they actually were. They argued that the press should have played down the terrorism, in order to offer the public a more accurate perspective on the threat. Instead, the press had taken a natural fear among the public and done what it could to make it worse. Fear, like war, sells newspapers.

Defenders of the press maintained that it had done no more than point out a real danger. There is no way to determine who was right. There is no objective standard to determine when news coverage has been so excessive and sensational as to incite *disproportionate* fear among the public. But clearly there is such a point, and fearmongering, for profit or any other reason, is an ethical concern.

DRAWING LINES

At times the line between news and entertainment is hard to find, even for the people who produce them. This is particularly true when it comes to television. The NBC and ABC television networks each have a morning show made up of news and weather reports, interviews with celebrities, and other features. Except for the personalities of the on-air regulars, the two shows are virtually indistinguishable in most respects. And yet, one is produced under the auspices of its network's news division, while the other is produced by its network's entertainment division.

The line between TV entertainers and TV newspeople can be equally hard to locate. Even Edward R. Murrow, easily the most respected of the early television newsmen, had a television series called *Person to Person*, which was essentially an entertainment show consisting of celebrity interviews. Many of today's TV newspeople have appeared in entertainment movies or television shows, usually playing themselves.

Journalists from all the media are to be found regularly on national television and in a variety of roles. Sometimes in the traditional journalistic role of interviewing others, but often being interviewed themselves, appearing as celebrities in their own right. At other times, they are there as salespeople, often for books or articles they have written, or for some other journalistic project they have been working on.

Although most network newspeople balk at doing commercials for retail products, local radio newspeople are routinely required to read commercials along with their news copy. And virtually all prominent television newspeople are expected, as a condition of their jobs, to appear in promotional spots for their own news programs. When they do, they are literally selling the news—or at least the news shows.

They are also selling themselves. And the more successful they are at selling themselves to the public, the higher the price they can command in the marketplace. In other words, the greater their personal celebrity—the more popular they become—the more money they can demand from their employers. Not only the news, but the newspeople themselves have become commodities.

Journalists differ about the extent to which these practices present them with ethical problems. Some find little to worry about in any of them. They see no reason why journalists should not be entertainers, or even salespeople, as well—provided that they do not let their various roles interfere with each other.

Others find any practice that turns a journalist into a public figure ethically troubling. They believe that a journalist should be a neutral conduit for information, not a celebrity. The personality—and ego—of the journalist can only get in the way of public understanding of the news, not enhance it.

A FUNDAMENTAL
CONFLICT?

In an earlier chapter, we talked about how money can present individual reporters with personal conflicts of interest. But money—the commercialism inherent in the "news business"—may present American journalism itself with a conflict of interest.

The whole thrust of commercialism is to make money, to sell newspapers, to get high ratings—to be *popular.* The basic function of journalism, on the other hand, is to tell the truth, whatever that truth may be, and however *unpopular* it may be. Those two goals would seem to be logically incompatible.

There is, then, a fundamental conflict of interest at the heart of American journalism. It is a tension that plays a part in many, if not most, of the ethical problems discussed in this book. To some extent, that tension is inescapable. American journalism grew up in commercialism, and it is—at least for the foreseeable future—firmly tied to it. But it is a tension of which thoughtful journalists, concerned with the ethics of their profession, must be aware—and beware.

NOTES

CHAPTER ONE

1. *Statistical Abstract of the United States,* 1986 edition, p. 545.
2. "Business Week/Harris Poll," *Business Week,* January 23, 1984, p. 24.
3. For a detailed discussion of the power of the American press to affect events, see Michael Kronenwetter's *Politics and the Press* (New York: Franklin Watts, 1987).

CHAPTER TWO

1. Commission on Freedom of the Press, *A Free and Responsible Press* (Chicago: University of Chicago Press, 1947).
2. The A.S.N.E Statement of Principles is reprinted in its entirety in Bruce M. Swain's *Reporters' Ethics* (Ames: Iowa State University Press, 1978), pp. 111-112.

CHAPTER THREE

1. These and the other statistics in this chapter describing editors' attitudes toward possible conflicts of interest are taken from "Newsroom Ethics: How Tough Is Enforcement?," an A.S.N.E. Ethics Committee Report (1986).
2. Charles W. Bailey, *Conflicts of Interest: A Matter of Journalistic Ethics* (Minneapolis: Minnesota Journalism Center, 1984), p. 19.
3. Some typical examples of this kind of puffery can be found in Tom Goldstein's *The News at Any Cost* (New York: Simon & Schuster, 1985), pp. 91-92.
4. The Winans affair is described in Goldstein, pp. 248-252, which also discusses the ethics of the way the *Wall Street Journal* reported the story.

CHAPTER FOUR

1. Susan Lindee and Dorothy Nelkin, "Challenger: The High Cost of Hype," *Bulletin of the Atomic Scientists,* November 1986, pp. 16-18.
2. *Time,* May 9, 1977, p. 22.
3. See Carl Bernstein and Bob Woodward, *All the President's Men* (New York: Simon & Schuster, 1974).
4. Testimony before the House Foreign Operations Subcommittee, United States House of Representatives, March 11, 1987.
5. The *Post*'s code is reprinted in its entirety in Swain, pp. 131-134.
6. Swain, p. 116.
7. These and other cases of journalists protecting their sources are reported in John L. Hulteng's *The Messenger's Motives* (Englewood Cliffs, N.J.: Prentice-Hall, 1976), pp. 98-99.
8. Hulteng, *The Messenger's Motives,* p. 99.

CHAPTER FIVE

1. Frank Luther Mott, *American Journalism 1690-1960,* 3rd edition (New York: Macmillan, 1962), p. 721.

CHAPTER SIX

1. Allen Churchill, *The Improper Bohemians* (New York: Ace Books, 1959), pp. 97-102.
2. William H. Marnell, *The Right to Know* (New York: Seabury Press, 1973), pp. 38-41.
3. Ron Dorfman, "Choking Off Information Through Prosecution," *The Quill,* December 1985, pp. 8-9.
4. Swain, p. 55. The Bay of Pigs case is discussed in more detail in Herbert Brucker's *Communication Is Power* (New York: Oxford University Press, 1973), pp. 42-44.
5. Personal conversation with the author, September 6, 1986.

CHAPTER SEVEN

1. Swain, p. 132.
2. Quoted by Eugene L. Roberts, Jr., in "On Collision Course," *The Quill,* April 1985, p. 18.
3. For a detailed discussion of the Westmoreland and Sharon cases, see *Reckless Disregard: Westmoreland v. CBS, et. al., Sharon v. "Time",* by Renata Adler. (New York: Knopf, 1986). No detailed account of the Burnett case is available.
4. Roberts. p. 18. This was the same Judge Bork later nominated to the Supreme Court by President Reagan and rejected by the Senate.
5. Steinem's article, "A Bunny's Tale," was originally published in two parts in *Show* magazine, in 1963. It was reprinted, with a postscript, 20 years later in Steinem's book *Outrageous Acts and Everyday Rebellions* (New York: Holt, Rinehart, 1983).
6. John Howard Griffin, *Black Like Me* (New York: Houghton Mifflin, 1961).

7. "Ethics, Bias, Accuracy: Fresh Attacks on TV News." *U.S. News & World Report*, September 5, 1983, p. 55.
8. Goldstein, p. 130.
9. The Janet Cooke affair is described at some length in "The Case of Janet Cooke," *Commentary*, August 1981, pp. 46-50.
10. Some of these devices are described in Hulteng, pp. 199-220, and the issue is explored at length in Goldstein, pp. 220-227.
11. Swain, pp. 115-116.
12. Only 15 percent of editors quizzed by the A.S.N.E. in 1983 said their papers had a regular ombudsman column.

CHAPTER EIGHT

1. See *The People and the Press, A Times-Mirror Investigation of Public Attitudes Toward the News Media*, conducted by the Gallup Organization, 1986.
2. Quoted by Dinesh D'Souza in "Accuracy in Media," *National Review*, November 2, 1984, p. 36.

CHAPTER NINE

1. Mott, pp. 222-224, 233, 297.
2. *San Francisco Chronicle*, March 6, 1969. Quoted in Brucker, p. 217.
3. *Miami Herald*, May 3, 1987, p. 1.
4. "The Sudden Fall of Gary Hart," *Newsweek*, May 18, 1987, pp. 22-28.
5. *Newsweek*, May 18, 1987, p. 25.
6. Quoted in "Your Story, but My Life," *Time*, December 12, 1983, p. 84.
7. Reported by Art Nauman, ombudsman of the *Sacramento Bee*, as quoted by Richard P. Cunningham, in "Fit for TV, But Not for Newspapers?," *The Quill*, April 1986, p. 7.
8. Quoted by J.R. Swearingen in his talk entitled "Responsibility in Journalism," delivered at the Conference on the Responsibilities of Journalism, University of Notre Dame, November 22, 1982 (reprinted in *Vital Speeches of the Day*, March 15, 1983).

BIBLIOGRAPHY

Altheide, David L. *Creating Reality: How TV News Distorts Events*. Beverly Hills, Calif.: Sage, 1976.

Bailey, Charles W. *Conflicts of Interest: A Matter of Journalistic Ethics*. A report to the National News Council. Minneapolis: Minnesota Journalism Center, 1984.

Brucker, Herbert. *Communication Is Power*. New York: Oxford University Press, 1973.

Cirino, Robert. *Don't Blame the People: How the News Media Uses Bias, Distortion and Censorship to Manipulate Public Opinion*. New York: Random House, 1972.

Commission on Freedom of the Press. *A Free and Responsible Press*. Chicago: University of Chicago Press, 1947.

Dorfman, Ron. "Choking Off Information Through Prosecution." *The Quill*, December 1985.

"Ethics, Bias, Accuracy: Fresh Attacks on TV News." *U.S. News & World Report*, September 5, 1983.

Fallows, James. "The New Celebrities of Washington." *The New York Review of Books*, June 12, 1986.

Fry, Don, ed. *Believing the News*. St. Petersburg, Fla.: Poynter Institute for Media Studies, 1985.

Goldstein, Tom. *The News at Any Cost*. New York: Simon & Schuster, 1985.

Griffith, Thomas. "The Pulitizer Hoax—Who Can be Believed?" *Time*, May 4, 1981.

Henry, William A. III, and others. "Journalism Under Fire." *Time*, December 12, 1983.

Hohenberg, John. *Free Press/Free People, the Best Cause*. New York: Columbia University Press, 1971.

Hulteng, John L. *The Messenger's Motives*. Englewood Cliffs, N.J.: Prentice Hall, 1976.

Kronenwetter, Michael. *Politics and the Press*. New York: Watts, 1987.

Marnell, William H. *The Right to Know*. New York: Seabury Press, 1973.

McGaffin, William, and Erwin Knoll. *Anything But the Truth, the Credibility Gap—How the News Is Managed in Washington*. New York: Putnam, 1968.

Merrill, John C., and Ralph D. Barney, eds. *Ethics and the Press: Readings in Mass Media Morality*. New York: Macmillan, 1975.

Mott, Frank Luther. *American Journalism, 1690–1960*. New York: Macmillan, 1962.

"Newsroom Ethics: How Tough Is Enforcement?" An A.S.N.E. Ethics Committee Report [undated], available from the American Society of Newspaper Editors, Washington, D.C.

Nimmo, Dan, and James E. Combs. *Nightly Horrors: Crisis Coverage by Television Network News*. Knoxville: University of Tennessee Press, 1985.

Paletz, David L., and Robert M. Entman. *Media Power Politics*. New York: The Free Press, 1981.

Pollard. James. *The Presidents and the Press*. New York: Macmillan, 1947.

Powell, Jody. *The Other Side of the Story*. New York: Morrow, 1984.

Ranney, Austin. *Channels of Power: The Impact of Television on American Politics*. New York: Basic Books, 1983.

Shaw, David. *Press Watch*. New York: Macmillan, 1984.

Swain, Bruce M. *Reporters Ethics*. Ames: Iowa State University Press, 1978.

Weisman, John. "Betrayal and Trust: The Tricky Art of Finding—and Keeping—Good TV News Sources." *TV Guide*, March 7, 1987.

INDEX

ABOUT THE AUTHOR

Michael Kronenwetter is a free-lance writer who wears many hats. He is a newspaper columnist and media critic who has also written award-winning filmstrips and radio plays.

Mr. Kronenwetter attended Northwestern University and the University of Wisconsin. His books include a history of the region of central Wisconsin where he was raised and now makes his home, and six other books for Franklin Watts: *Are You a Liberal? Are You a Conservative?*, *Free Press v. Fair Trial: Television and Other Media in the Courtroom*, *Capitalism vs. Socialism: Economic Policies of the U.S. and U.S.S.R.*, *The Threat from Within: Unethical Politics and Politicians*, *Politics and the Press*, and *The Military Power of the President*.